6 Report

People, Place, and Purpose: Churches and Neighbourhood Resilience in the North East

Paul Bickley

Theos – enriching conversations

Theos exists to enrich the conversation about the role of faith in society.

Religion and faith have become key public issues in this century, nationally and globally. As our society grows more religiously diverse, we must grapple with religion as a significant force in public life. All too often, though, opinions in this area are reactionary or ill informed.

We exist to change this

We want to help people move beyond common misconceptions about faith and religion, behind the headlines and beneath the surface. Our rigorous approach gives us the ability to express informed views with confidence and clarity.

As the UK's leading religion and society think tank, we reach millions of people with our ideas. Through our reports, events and media commentary, we influence today's influencers and decision makers. According to *The Economist*, we're "an organisation that demands attention". We believe Christianity can contribute to the common good and that faith, given space in the public square, will help the UK to flourish.

Will you partner with us?

Theos receives no government, corporate or denominational funding. We rely on donations from individuals and organisations to continue our vital work. Please consider signing up as a Theos Friend or Associate or making a one off donation today.

Theos Friends and Students

— Stay up to date with our monthly newsletter

— Receive (free) printed copies of our reports

— Get free tickets to all our events

£75/ year
for Friends

£40/ year
for Students

Theos Associates

— Stay up to date with our monthly newsletter

— Receive (free) printed copies of our reports

— Get free tickets to all our events

— Get invites to private events with the Theos team and other Theos Associates

£375/ year

Sign up on our website:
www.theosthinktank.co.uk/about/support-us

Contents

Contents

Acknowledgements

This research is the result of a William Leech Research Fellowship. These Fellowships were established in 1988 to support high-quality research projects in the area of Christian social ethics and practical theology in the North East of England. Grants are made for projects that engage with the people and churches of the region, develop theological reflection on practice, and seek to create social impact from dissemination of the research. We at Theos are grateful to the Management Committee of the William Leech Research Fellowship for their support and encouragement.

We are also indebted to the residents and churches of our case study neighbourhoods in Byker, Shildon and North Ormesby. Areas of high deprivation are the subject of many research projects, and all have been patient, accommodating, hospitable and honest. We hope that this work and what comes after will be of value to them.

I am extremely grateful for the support of the Theos staff team (including former colleague Jennie Pollock for copy-editing this report). I am particularly indebted to Research Assistant Charlotte Hobson. Charlotte arrived at Theos one day and was assisting with fieldwork in Shildon the next. Her support in the closing stages of this project has been invaluable.

Paul Bickley

August 2018

Executive summary

The research

As part of a William Leech Research Fellowship looking at the role of churches in building resilience in the North East we set out to:

— Explore the theme of 'resilience', particularly with a view to asking whether religious institutions have or have not been included in traditional models, and why.

— Bring the idea of community and neighbourhood resilience into dialogue with theological reflection around the ministry of local churches, looking to find both the resonances and dissonances.

— Offer a theologically-informed definition of resilience, building on insights from social science perspectives, and setting the parameters of subsequent work.

— Engage three churches in the North East in a programme of participative research. This research would look to uncover how congregations think and act when it comes to the challenge of achieving greater resilience.

— Reflect on how Christian ideas of suffering, endurance and hope tangibly shape the ministry of churches in areas of high deprivation and contribute to a wider resilience in the community.

— Develop proposals on how churches and policy makers could recognise the public significance of the ministry of churches, crystallised around the theme of resilience.

The research was carried out through an extensive literature survey on the theme of resilience (see Appendix 2), desk research around the vulnerabilities and risks facing communities in the North East, and three case studies of neighbourhoods/churches in the North East: Byker, Shildon, and North Ormesby.

Context

The North East has an undeserved reputation of being economically and socially depressed. Regional leaders reject the narrative of decline. The region has a strong identity and an important role to play in national economy and culture.

However, the North East faces multiple challenges. It has a higher concentration of deprived neighbourhoods than anywhere other than London. The North East is especially vulnerable to the potential ill-effects of Britain's departure from the European Union. Alongside national, regional, economic and political measures, a neighbourhood-level response is required.

The North East has a strong identity and an important role to play in national economy and culture.

Local civic and social action can make a difference between a community remaining liveable and entering into serious decline. In the past, governments have built a range of policy interventions around neighbourhoods. This neighbourhood-based approach has been largely abandoned, to the detriment of deprived communities.

Resilience

Resilience has been applied in a variety of different contexts, and is often used generically. On the one hand, it is attached to any public-spirited action after a trauma. On the other, language around 'bouncing' or 'snapping' back is unhelpful in a social context.

Neighbourhood resilience relies on three factors or domains: people, place, and purpose. These describe the combination of social capital (local voluntary action and leadership), physical capital (social infrastructure – common space), and spiritual capital (a neighbourhood's culture, morale, identity and meaning-making).

People

Social capital describes the levels of trust, reciprocity and cooperative action in a community. We draw attention to themes of individual support and care, volunteering and activism, and cooperation between institutional leaders.

Supporting individuals in appropriate ways – building their resilience – contributes to neighbourhood resilience in the long-run. Beneficiaries often became volunteers in turn. Churches valued 'with and alongside' rather than 'to and for' models of community action, though some struggled to break away from give-away charitable models.

Some churches were engaging large numbers of volunteers, often across racial and religious divides. Others, however, were more dependent on staff and a clergy, making projects difficult to sustain.

Neighbourhood resilience relies on three factors or domains: people, place, and purpose.

There was a diversity of community organisations in each case study neighbourhood with varying levels of collaboration between churches and others. Grassroots community action was sometimes seen to be unnecessarily fragmented.

Place

Physical spaces of gathering are important for neighbourhood resilience. There is concern that many deprived areas are losing such spaces.

Some churches have multi-purpose community buildings, the importance of which is hard to overestimate, particularly as other spaces of gathering (pubs, community centres, youth clubs) are closing. Ensuring communities have such spaces is a key future priority.

However, simply having spaces that are open to the community is not enough. If they are not properly used they can fail to be places that genuinely build relationship. Additionally, churches have spaces that don't readily lend themselves to community service or community development purposes. Churches were running extensive community services from improvised or shop front spaces. They were hampered by the small size and lack of versatility of these facilities.

Physical spaces of gathering are important for neighbourhood resilience. There is concern that many deprived areas are losing such spaces.

Purpose

Relatively deprived communities are often dominated by narratives of decline. These stories contain elements of truth but they also trap areas in their own past and prevent adaption and learning. They are resistance stories rather than resilience stories, 'if only' stories rather than 'what if' stories. This low or negative 'spiritual capital' can result in insularity, low aspiration, and disengagement. In other words, it damages resilience.

Churches are well-placed to build 'spiritual capital' by tackling decline stories with meaningful celebration, internal diversity and a focus on the possibility of change over time.

Key recommendations

The report argues that resilience, as understood through the domains of people, place and purpose, should re-shape thinking on church-based social action in the future.

It makes 12 recommendations, listed in full in the conclusion. These include:

— Resilience tools should be used by churches at a neighbourhood, regional and national level to support their community action, resource allocation, and vocational training. Churches should move away from give-away charitable models, focus on the training and development of local leaders, and collaborate more closely with other community organisations through formal neighbourhood partnerships.

Churches are well-placed to build 'spiritual capital' by tackling decline stories with meaningful celebration, internal diversity and a focus on the possibility of change over time.

— Local authorities should conduct neighbourhood audits of community facilities, using them to build on and support facilities that are already there, including churches. Public authorities should work harder to make their own facilities available for grassroots community use and churches need to work harder to make churches more suitable for community use.

— To make significant new funds available, a new Community Wealth Fund could be established. A Shale

Wealth Fund is already being developed to support communities near shale gas extraction sites. The Community Wealth Fund could be funded through multiple sources: the proposed post-Brexit shared prosperity fund, dormant assets, or an endowment.

— Churches are well positioned to help build an inclusive and positive national identity and should be engaging with conversations around culture and identity as enthusiastically as they do on issues of poverty and exclusion.

Preface

Resilience has been defined as:

> *the capacity of individuals [or communities] to navigate their way to the psychological, social, cultural, and physical resources that sustain their well-being and their capacity individually and collectively to negotiate for these resources to be provided in culturally meaningful ways.*[1]

The language of resilience – which is often rightly criticised as being too vague and imprecise – has nevertheless become important in a variety of disciplines seeking to negotiate challenging new circumstances. Global market forces, climate change, and sheer political unpredictability have forced a reappraisal. In the words of one author in the international development sector, "we do not have intellectual tools to understand how these [emerging factors] affect development".[2] In the development world, the turn to resilience arises out of a need to help communities survive – or even thrive – in the context of new vulnerabilities.

There is an obvious analogy with the engagement of charities, voluntary groups, and other helping organisations working in the domestic context of the UK. Climate change may not present the acute and immediate challenge that it does elsewhere (though in terms of civil resilience it clearly presents some). However, stark regional inequalities and the retrenchment of the state seen in the last decade present a chronic challenge to the flourishing of many communities – particularly those in the North East.

These challenges have also contributed to political disruption. Britain's intended departure from the European Union creates other risks, uncertainties and – no doubt – opportunities. The competence and capacity of the cash-starved public services to help people negotiate challenging circumstances is now in doubt, questioned in a way that it has not been for 30 years.

As civil society attempts to 'plug the gap', compassionate action has almost become a 'growth industry'. Churches and faith-based organisations are now accepted in the public square in a way that they were not a decade ago. While some suspicions remain, there has been a sufficient drip-feed of positive coverage of simple human kindness to warm the hearts of all but the most hardened secularists. Politically, the mood music has rarely been warmer. Christian compassionate action is now seen as an important (if not the most important) expression of Christian mission.

The question is, do we have the tools to understand and engage in the emerging conditions? The aim of this research has been to use the insights of resilience thinking to explore how church-based social action could face the challenges of the future. Is there a need for a similar paradigm shift in the UK? If there is, what would that shift look like? Our contention is that meeting needs – subsistence social action – is no longer enough. Churches can and should play a role in the promotion of community resilience.

Evidence from other parts of the world, where a resilience approach has been used by churches and faith-based organisations, suggest that there is a natural connection. For one thing, the religious views they promote can engender positivity and hope,

> As civil society attempts to 'plug the gap', compassionate action has almost become a 'growth industry'. Churches and faith-based organisations are now accepted in the public square in a way that they were not a decade ago.

offering individuals interpretive frameworks within which to understand their current struggles as meaningful. In doing so, religions can "equip individuals to withstand shock"[3]. Churches can be influential in aiding the development of relationships within and between communities. Sharing beliefs with others and participating in religious rituals and ceremonies can engender a shared identity and sense of belonging.[4] One outcome of this can be to 'bridge the gap' between individuals from differing backgrounds, social status and levels of privilege, offering opportunities for the disadvantaged to gain access to resources that would be hard for them to reach ordinarily.[5] So why hasn't resilience thinking been used by faith-based organisations in the domestic context?

This research offers a new way of thinking about the social action of churches and other neighbourhood faith institutions.

Through an analysis of the language of resilience, and three in-depth action research case studies, this research offers a new way of thinking about the social action of churches and other neighbourhood faith institutions. It is intended for anyone who takes an interest in how churches can best serve vulnerable communities. It will be of particular interest to those who are looking for a different perspective on place-based social action. We also draw contextual lessons for those who create the social architecture in which the churches and community organisations serve – be they denominational or public decision makers. Our hope is that this supports the work of churches and other faith-based organisations in the North East and hopefully beyond.

1   Michael Ungar, 'Resilience across Cultures', *The British Journal of Social Work*, Volume 38, Issue 2 (2008), p. 218–235.

2   Katrina Brown, *Resilience, Development and Global Change* (London: Routledge, 2016), p. xii.

3   Refugee Studies Centre, *Local Faith Communities and Resilience in Humanitarian Situations* (2013) p. 3. www.rsc.ox.ac.uk/files/files-1/wp90-local-faith-communities-resilience-2013.pdf

4   Yolanda Dreyer, 'Community resilience and spirituality – keys to hope for a post-apartheid South Africa' *Pastoral Psychology*, 64, 5 (2015), pp. 651-662 (p. 657); Refugee Studies Centre, *Local Faith Communities* (2013) p. 1.

5   Chloe Quanrud and Catriona Dejean, *Inspiring Change: Impact and Learning Report* (Tearfund, 2016) p. 16.

Introduction

INTRODUCTION SUMMARY

— The North East has an undeserved reputation of being economically and socially depressed. Regional leaders reject the narrative of decline. The region has a strong identity and an important role to play in national economy and culture.

— However, the North East faces multiple challenges. It has a higher concentration of deprived neighbourhoods than anywhere other than London. Local civic and social action can make a difference between a community remaining liveable and entering into serious decline.

— Neighbourhood resilience relies on factors around people, place, and purpose – a combination of social capital (local leadership), physical capital (enacted spaces), and spiritual capital (institutions and people that act according to hopeful, future-oriented stories).

Faith in troubled times

In May of 2014, a national newspaper ran a controversial feature piece: "The north-east of England: Britain's Detroit?"[1]

Detroit has become a morality tale of post-industrial failure. In July 2013, with debts estimated at $18–20 billion, the municipal authorities filed for bankruptcy. The bankruptcy was a final act in a long drama of decline including the collapse of the city's car manufacturing industry, a combination of joblessness and significant numbers employed in the public sector, a shrinking in population (1.8 million in 1950, down to 700,000 at the time of the bankruptcy), and the fragmentation of public services. Reports estimated that in 2013 there were 78,000 abandoned buildings in the city. The article implied that the North East was in a similar position.

One particularly trenchant response to the article began by citing 'Betteridge's Law' (any headline which ends in a question mark can be answered by the word 'no').[2] The North East is not Britain's Detroit. Why? Responses to the article pointed to a more positive selection of economic indicators, to the world-class universities, to a higher quality of life, to a growing digital sector, to the ongoing presence of a manufacturing sector, and so on. Leader of Newcastle City Council Nick Forbes lamented the way the article "chose to buy into a narrative of decline rather than reflecting what those of us who live here know – our better days are ahead of us rather than behind us".[3]

There is, however, at least something to be said in defence of the comparison. One of our interviewees – a community development worker from Hartlepool – spoke to us about a recently established community land trust in North Ormesby. He was reflecting on the fact that it cost more to acquire and restore a property than its actual market value.

> *What is the alternative to intervening in that way? It's the Detroit model I suppose, isn't it? You just let the market run away. You have empty, derelict properties, you have spiralling decline. And some would say the area becomes unviable, all the value has gone out of the land and property, so bulldoze the lot. That has happened, to some extent, just down the road in South Bank.*

Put in another way, different institutions in the neighbourhood had to make interventions that, in purely financial terms, were illogical. Why? For the sake of the area's 'liveability', and because without this the area could slide from already deprived into further decline.

The North East as a whole is not Detroit. There are, however, many neighbourhoods that exist on a threshold between a deprived but liveable community, and one where the pace of physical and social decline overtakes the ability of residents, local institutions and public services to resist. It is worth asking how such neighbourhoods are best helped – and if they can be better helped. Or perhaps, since even the most deprived areas possess people of goodwill, what are the ways of helping that can tip a neighbourhood into a virtuous cycle, and are there ways of helping which do not assist in that way at all?

What are the ways of helping that can tip a neighbourhood into a virtuous cycle?

The North East (along with London) has the greatest concentrations of deprived areas in the country (as a proportion of the number of local authorities within that region). How can neighbourhoods be helped and sustained in the face of such social change?

Our research

Increasingly the answer offered is 'resilience' – a term that is increasingly apparent in both public and academic discourse. The word is almost mystically flexible. It has been applied to individuals, with a view to enhancing psychological and emotional resilience, to economies buffeted by recession, and to disaster relief and community development work in the global South, in the sphere of civil resilience to fire and flood, and to businesses. Resilience is simply what is present when people or systems do better than might be expected under the circumstances – an appealing concept for any context when unpredictability, complexity and change are the norm. In such disciplines, building resilience is the best way of preparing for the many eventualities of uncertain times.

The turn to resilience is prompted by a desire to shape systems or actions in ways that reflect risk, uncertainty and change – and while risk, uncertainty and change are facts of life, they are in many contexts being experienced more sharply (in the global South for instance, climate change is perhaps the most significant driver of resilience thinking).

Similar questions are being asked in the context of community development in the UK. What responses to poverty and deprivation are appropriate in a post-crash and post-austerity environment where public services have been curtailed and the neighbourhood renewal agenda of the first decade of this century more or less abandoned? Answer: community resilience. For instance, in 2011 the Churches Regional Commission in the North East published *Community resilience: a necessary ingredient in difficult times.*[4] This helpful – but currently not publicly available – research was built around case studies in Jarrow and Walker, and addressed a range of issues from economic resilience to political extremism (making a connection between low levels of resilience and support for the British National Party).

> **Building resilience is the best way of preparing for the many eventualities of uncertain times.**

Resilience is an answer to an important set of questions, but is it the right answer? If being all things to all men is the core of its appeal then this same flexibility represents a serious flaw – it makes it analytically weak, and therefore not necessarily helpful in shaping action. Some criticise the banality of the way it is used: "what was once referred to as putting down sand bags to stop flooding or ensuring that there are separate toilets for men and women are now described as resilience measures."[5] If resilience can mean almost anything, it runs the risk of meaning almost nothing. If it doesn't mean much, it is hardly a helpful frame for interventions.

This is the background for this report, which sets out findings from a William Leech Research Fellowship looking at the role of churches in building resilience in the North East. We set out to:

— Explore the theme of 'resilience', particularly with a view to asking whether religious institutions have or have not been included in traditional models, and why.

— Bring the idea of community and neighbourhood resilience into dialogue with theological reflection around the ministry of local churches, looking to find both the resonances and dissonances.

— Offer a theologically-informed definition of resilience, building on insights from social science perspectives, and setting the parameters of subsequent work;

— Engage three churches in the North East in a programme of participative research. This research would look to uncover how congregations think and act when it comes to the challenge of achieving greater resilience.

— Reflect on how Christian ideas of suffering, endurance and hope tangibly shape the ministry of churches in areas of high deprivation and contribute to a wider resilience in the community.

— Develop proposals on how churches and policy makers could recognise the public significance of the ministry of churches, crystallised around the theme of resilience.

Our intended outcome is to help churches engage with ideas around resilience and use it to build skills, experience, and insight into their public role. We want to encourage, challenge and resource churches in the North East (and beyond) as well as provoke change in the wider social and political context.

Report structure

Chapter 1 offers context to the research, setting out some of the principal political, social and economic challenges faced in the North East before turning to a deeper discussion of the idea of resilience. Drawing on some of the key themes in existing literature and our empirical case studies we identify three key components of resilience: social, physical, and spiritual capital (see a brief introduction to these themes in this section below).

Chapters 2, 3 and 4 consider the importance of social, physical, and spiritual capital in turn, unpacking the ways in which they respectively help people act together, adapt to change, and attach meaning to vulnerability and struggle. Each chapter will offer a brief theoretical background and will draw on examples from the respective empirical case studies in Byker,

Our intended outcome is to help churches engage with ideas around resilience and use it to build skills, experience, and insight into their public role. We want to encourage, challenge and resource churches in the North East (and beyond) as well as provoke change in the wider social and political context.

Shildon and North Ormesby. Interviews are anonymised, but where unavoidable (specifically in the chapter on place) we have identified the case study area.

The report will then conclude with recommendations relevant for local churches and national denominations, but also local and national decision makers.

The report includes appendices with case study neighbourhood profiles and an extended survey of the theoretic material around resilience.

Resilience – a brief discussion

Many commentators argue that resilience language is used in superficial or facile ways. Indeed, it has been argued that in some ways it is actively misleading and harmful. If that is the case, then resilience can't help us understand communities or shape practical action.

Before we move to our discussion of why resilience is important, and in view of the sheer elasticity of the term, readers deserve an early look at exactly what we're talking about.

Basic etymology gives us a place to start. Martin et al set out the following basic meanings.

> — *Resilience – resilire: to resume form and function elastically following a disturbance*

> — *Resilience as **"bounce-back"** to [a] pre-shock state or path – "speed of recovery"*

> — *Resilience as **"ability to absorb"** shocks – "stability of structure and function"*

> — *Resilience as* **"robustness"** *- [the] capacity to maintain*
> *core system performance through* **"adaptability of**
> **structure and function"** [6]

Here we have clarity, but of course these can only help us so far in thinking about the social world. Human communities aren't really comparable to materials, structures or systems. On the other hand, it will not do to suggest that resilience is a 'know it when you see it' kind of a thing. If resilience is to be a useful set of ideas, it should be sufficiently specific to help us do things like measure it, describe the contribution of different factors, or identify ways in which it can be developed.

Most resilience research looks to identify a series of protective factors that together make for a resilient system. For instance, a study of four communities in Sheffield highlights 1) a basic infrastructure of public places that encourages gathering and collaboration; 2) an inclusive sense of belonging; 3) information, voice and power, and; 4) community infrastructure and action.[7] The Churches Regional Commission in the North East's work identifies five 'building blocks' of resilient communities: community economic development, political engagement, community social capital, structural and environmental matters, and individuals in community – and alongside these an array of other positive/protective factors.

If the purpose of talking about resilience is to help communities become more resilient, then most definitions are too simplistic, or indeed too complicated to seek to apply. We favour an approach that is both comprehensive and relatively simple: neighbourhood resilience relies on the presence of *social* capital, *physical* capital and *spiritual* capital. We describe these three domains as people, place and purpose.

Social capital relates to the networks of friendship, reciprocity and institutional life. Physical capital relates to spaces of public gathering and public action. Spiritual capital describes the stories, identities and cultures that dominate in any neighbourhood.

These things will be present in all communities, though it is widely acknowledged that not all forms of social capital, for instance, are necessarily positive. Equally, physical capital may be fragile (i.e., a lack of buildings, or buildings that don't really work effectively) and there may be a deficit of spiritual capital (the ability to tell hopeful stories about a neighbourhood's present and future). These themes will be explained in depth in the next chapter.

Before that, however, we set out the factors that make the task of building resilience such a pressing one.

Social capital relates to the networks of friendship, reciprocity and institutional life. Physical capital relates to spaces of public gathering and public action. Spiritual capital describes the stories, identities and cultures that dominate in any neighbourhood.

1   Andy Beckett, 'The north-east of England: Britain's Detroit?', *The Guardian*, 10 May 2014 www.theguardian.com/uk-news/2014/may/10/north-east-avoid-becoming-britains-detroit

2   Paul Smith, 'Lies, damned lies, statistics—and The Guardian', *Medium*, 11 May 2014 medium.com/@paul_a_smith/lies-damned-lies-statistics-and-the-guardian-7f4f88ade648

3   Nick Forbes in Letters, *The Guardian*, 12 May 2014 www.theguardian.com/uk-news/2014/may/12/positive-portrait-north-east-england

4   Following the dissolution of the Churches' Regional Commission for the North East in 2015, this document is no longer publicly available. Thanks to Jim Robertson, former chief officer of the Commission, for sharing these documents with us. Although our research covers much of the same ground, the work of the CRC for the North East only tangentially considers the role of churches in supporting resilience.

5   Jonathan Joseph, 'Resilience as embedded neoliberalism: a governmentality approach', *Resilience*, 1:1 (2013), p. 50. DOI: 10.1080/21693293.2013.765741

6   R Martin, P Sunley, B Gardiner and P Tyler, 'Resilience and Local Economic Growth Paths', presentation for the Cambridge Local Economic Growth Conference, July 2013. www.geog.cam.ac.uk/research/projects/cger/conference/7martin.pdf

7   Deborah Platts-Fowler and David Robinson, 'Community resilience: a policy tool for local government?' *Local Government Studies* 42:5 (2016) p. 4.

1
Context

CHAPTER 1 SUMMARY

— The conversation around resilience in the North East is a response to perceived risks. The North East faces a particularly difficult combination of economic, social and political challenges. The region faces particular vulnerabilities because of Britain's exit from the European Union.

— The importance of local, neighbourhood-level responses to these vulnerabilities is set out. Neighbourhood incorporates objective physical geography and a subjective perception of network and identity. In the past, governments have built a range of policy interventions around neighbourhoods, these have been abandoned to the detriment of deprived communities.

— Resilience can be under- or over-defined. On the one hand, it is attached to any public-spirited action after a trauma. On the other, language around 'bouncing' or 'snapping' back is unhelpful in a social context. The importance of ideas of learning, adaption, and collective action are highlighted as significant.

— Churches have reserves of the things that make for neighbourhood resilience – social capital, physical capital, and spiritual capital. We call these people, places, and purpose.

Resilient to what?

The North East faces a series of significant challenges, many of them with national – even global – causes. There is nothing novel about that. What is new perhaps is the heady cocktail of economic, social and political challenges that increasingly reinforce each other.

The over-supply of steel from the state-run Chinese steel industry that contributed to the closure of the SSI steel plant in Redcar in 2015 is one such example. Overnight, 3,000 more people found themselves out of work in an area of already high unemployment. To add insult to injury, the cash-strapped local authority was also a creditor of the company, and was left with £10.7 million of unpaid debt.[1]

The North East, or at least parts of it, is subject to what could be called "multiple overwhelmings", in theologian David Ford's phrase (an idea to which we will return).[2] For now, we briefly summarise these economic, social and political challenges.

Economic change

It is often said the North East's economy is insufficiently resilient. Cuts in state spending (which has seen the loss of 400,000 jobs in the North as a whole since 2010) have had their impact, as has the decline of heavy manufacturing. While it retains a relatively high quotient of jobs in research and development, chemicals and car manufacturing, only one in ten jobs in the North East is now in manufacturing.

According to the North East Local Economic Partnership, the region's economy faces two problems in particular. The first is low rates of employment. Its unemployment rate of 4.9% for the first quarter of 2018 is the highest of all English regions – although there have recently been signs of a decrease. The second problem – low productivity – is more entrenched. In 2016, the Gross Value Added (GVA) per head – a measure of productivity – of the North East Local Economic Partnership area was £19,658. This is well below the GVA per head of England excluding London (£23,659) and England as a whole (£27,060).[3]

There are likely multiple causes of low productivity. Commentators point to a lack of consistent investment in public infrastructure and skills (for example, public spending on transport in the North East in 2016/17 was £291 per head, compared to the national average of £425 and a figure for London of £944 per head). They also point to low wages and lacklustre wage growth – last year real wages were still 3.3% lower than in 2007 across the North as a whole, both factors which tend to contribute to low productivity.

A recent report from IPPR North sets out the human cost:

> [There are] 2 million working-age people living in households below the poverty line, 300,000 more than there were in 2003/4–2005/6 – an increase of 17.6 per cent... In the North East, this figure increased by a third (33.3 per cent) – the largest increase in the country alongside the West Midlands.[4]

The North East Child Poverty Commission found that 24% of children in the region live in poverty (above the national average of 21%). The Institute for Fiscal Studies predicts that this will grow worse in the next few years, and more markedly in already poor areas and for families that are dependent on benefits for the majority of their income.[5]

Educational inequalities are correlated with socio-economic factors and start before children enter primary school. While primary school performance in the North East is generally good (schools in some areas excel in helping disadvantaged pupils attain a good standard) attainment in the secondary sector is less good. On

Educational inequalities are correlated with socio-economic factors and start before children enter primary school.

raw exam results, no area in the North East matches even the London average, though other measures paint a more positive picture.[6]

Social and economic deprivation also drives health inequalities, which place further pressure on public services and welfare spending. Regionally, for instance, 7.9% claim employment support allowance and incapacity benefits, compared to 6.1% nationally. Healthy life expectancy for men in the North East is 59.7 years – 6.2 years less than for men in the South East. For women, healthy life expectancy in the North East is 59.8 years – 6.8 years less than in the South East.

Demographic change

Like nearly all areas of the United Kingdom, the North East has an ageing population. Unlike most other areas, however, the North East – along with the North West – is projected to see an actual fall in the number of 16- to 65-year-olds in the ten years to 2026.[7] The Office for National Statistics predicts that by 2041 the North East will have a higher old age dependency ratio (OADR) than many other parts of the country.[8] Some commentators have also pointed out that the future old will be less wealthy and less able to help sustain local economies.

> Social and economic deprivation also drives health inequalities, which place further pressure on public services and welfare spending.

Additionally, there is expected to be negligible natural population change in the region in the next decade. Projections for the period 2016-2026 suggest a growth of 50,000. However, only 1,000 of this will come from 'natural' growth. A much higher proportion (44,000 in fact) will be net international migration. This is an economic and social necessity, and arguably a social good, but also a significant social challenge. It may contribute to a sense – occasionally mentioned by interviewees – that more affluent parts of the country are 'exporting' social challenges to the North East. Of the 99 Local Authority areas that have agreed to asylum seeker dispersal, only 33 have more than one asylum seeker per 1,000 residents. In Middlesbrough, Glasgow, Rochdale, Stockton-on-Tees and Bolton the proportion is more than one in 300. In 2015 Middlesbrough breached the "cluster limit" of no more than one asylum seeker per 200 residents.[9]

So the North East will become markedly more diverse, which has implications for the cohesiveness of communities. To take asylum seeker dispersal as an example, in spite of the often complex needs of asylum seekers, no extra money comes from central government for schools, hospitals or other public services. Dispersals are carried out by private contractors and asylum seekers are housed in private accommodation without any coordination with the local authority. These are fertile conditions for a building sense of resentment – the already stretched having to take on another burden.

Political change

Fifty eight per cent of the region voted to exit the European Union, in places by a significant margin (e.g., in Hartlepool 69.6% voted for departure). As with many Brexit-supporting areas, this comes in spite of the fact that the region is a net beneficiary of EU spending, and that a significant part of the North East's trade is with the Euro-zone. In fact, the North East is alone amongst English regions in having a positive balance of trade with the EU. In 2015 the region sent £7 billion of goods to the EU – 58% of total North East exports and well above the UK average of 48%.[10]

On both counts, it is more vulnerable than other English regions to potential negative outcomes of Britain's departure from the European Union (EU). It is claimed that 160,000 jobs in the region rely on trade with the EU. Leaked government forecasts suggest that even if there is a comprehensive trade deal, then GDP could shrink by 11%. Without such a deal, regional GDP could shrink by as much as 16%. If it is the case that the region has only recently and partially recovered from the 2008 recession, and with retrenchment of public services, then the consequences of such a change are hard to imagine, particularly for areas which have not really benefitted from the limited return to prosperity within the region.

Meanwhile, the regional devolution agenda is developing in the region. The North East was once a testing ground for New Labour's ideas of regional assemblies. The proposals were rejected in a referendum in 2004, by 78% to 22%. Yet the question of regional level governance returned after 2010 with the 'northern powerhouse' agenda and city-based devolution deals.

The North East Combined Authority – an association for the seven councils which serve the North East: County Durham, Gateshead, Newcastle, North Tyneside, Northumberland, South Tyneside and Sunderland – recently voted in favour of a 'North of Tyne' devolution deal for Newcastle, North Tyneside and Northumberland. The deal includes plans for a directly elected Mayor for North of Tyne and £600 million of extra money for investment, amongst other commitments.

The move is controversial, coming just two years after the scrapping of a region-wide devolution plan. Other councils in the region only grudgingly supported the move. The leader of Gateshead council abstained and criticised the deal for insufficient devolution of powers and funding. Only time will tell if the deal is well-conceived. Either way, there is a question over where it leaves other parts of the region, and whether it reinforces historic tensions between the north and south of the Tyne.

What is the right response?

The North East shouldn't be portrayed as a post-industrial, downtrodden rustbelt. The region has strengths as well as vulnerabilities. However, it does face serious economic, social and political challenges, which are sharpened by Britain's departure from the EU. These regional vulnerabilities are compounded by local challenges which vary from place to place.

> The North East shouldn't be portrayed as a post-industrial, downtrodden rustbelt. The region has strengths as well as vulnerabilities. However, it does face serious economic, social and political challenges, which are sharpened by Britain's departure from the EU.

How can the region best respond to these multiple difficulties?

One strategy is to build the regional economy. Measures could include building transport infrastructure or improving the skills base in the area. Some of this could happen, and is happening, through existing agencies. The North East Local Economic Partnership (NELEP), one of 38 LEPs across the country, has a strategic plan to tackle some of the structural issues mentioned above. Other strategies would require a substantial change in priorities or powers at the central of local government level.

The post-Brexit 'Shared Prosperity Fund' will in theory contribute to attempts to reduce poverty through economic development. It is an open question whether this can be spent more effectively than the European Structural Fund (ESF) it is intended to replace. One of the criticisms of ESF is that the programme is primarily driven by national policy and doesn't allow for local participation or adjustment. A Local Enterprise Partnership-driven shared prosperity fund might well still be centralised, if only regionally. Marginal neighbourhoods, particularly those outside of major conurbations, could easily fail to benefit even from an effective and successful programme.

Another strategy is to look to high-level political change, restoring levels of public spending, a more generous welfare settlement and increased levels of public investment. Of course, most of the North East consistently votes for Labour (only four Parliamentary seats returned Conservative MPs in the 2017 general election) implying that voters in the region would prefer a different political direction. However, it is not clear that a future change in government would result in a substantial reinvestment in local services – though it would superficially appear otherwise, the pressure on public services is systemic rather than political. The North of Tyne devolution deal comes with some extra powers and some extra money, but they are limited, and clearly leave outstanding questions with regard to the southern half of the region.

Other kinds of responses are required to complement those above.

A neighbourhood-level response

Regional GVA, rates of employment, the outcome of the Brexit negotiations – in other words, the big regional drivers of standards of living – are what they are, and won't directly be changed by neighbourhood-level action. People will, however, experience their effects at a local – more specifically, at a neighbourhood – level.

As Ed Cox, former director of IPPR North observes in his report, *Love thy Neighbourhood: People and Place in Social Reform*, the first decade of the new millennium was a significant one for neighbourhood-based government initiatives. A succession of neighbourhood-led programmes – the New Deal for Communities, National Strategy for Neighbourhood Renewal, Neighbourhood Renewal Fund and Working Neighbourhoods Fund – demonstrated that administration's attachment to neighbourhood-led policy. All highlighted the importance of neighbourhood and neighbourhood-level investment, as opposed to national measures, and had a goal of ensuring that "within 10 to 20 years no-one should be seriously disadvantaged by where they live".

Spending in each of the 39 New Deal for Communities (NDC) areas was substantial, amounting in some cases to over £50 million on locally determined priorities. The programme did not meet its lofty ambition of narrowing the gap between rich and poor neighbourhoods, but audits of the programme argued that it was cost-effective – specifically noting improved mental health outcomes. NDC areas also tended to be targeted by other programmes, the cumulative effect of which was genuine improvements in people's experience of these areas.

After 2010, the neighbourhood agenda faded – or certainly changed. The Coalition government explicitly championed the empowerment of communities through the 'Big Society'. This came in the form of new rights and powers – such as the

Localism Act's (2011) community asset transfers – rather than by investing resources. Since the Big Society was consigned to the scrap-heap of political rhetoric, the government's neighbourhood policy has been to encourage the Localism Act's new neighbourhood planning process and to enable privately financed housing redevelopment.[11]

Cox argues that Coalition (and, by extension, later Conservative) policy can be distinguished from what comes before in the following ways:

— There is very little particular focus on deprived neighbourhoods – programmes apply to all communities regardless of their capacity to use them, and few if any targets or indicators of success are in place.

— There is very little investment in physical regeneration, and what does take place is led by the private sector.

— Programmes largely depend on community initiative – they are supported by only very small sums of public money, and largely avoid or exclude local government and other state actors.[12]

Put simply, neighbourhoods as such are now no longer a target of government thinking or policy. Writing for the Joseph Rowntree Foundation, Alasdair Rae et al suggest that since 2010 the view has shifted even further than that. Regeneration should promote sustainable growth rather than 'prop up' areas allegedly in terminal decline. No longer did the government conceive of its role as creating jobs or encouraging investment in the most

Neighbourhoods as such are now no longer a target of government thinking or policy.

disadvantaged areas, a marked shift from the regional policy of the past. Rather, the task is to support areas best positioned for growth and encourage individuals to commute or move to these centres of opportunity.[13]

This is validated by the fact that, in comparison with a decade ago, work in this field is now extremely piecemeal. Probably the most consistent single investment in deprived communities has been non-governmental – the Local Trust's Big Local programme, which offered a £1 million grant across ten years to 150 areas (nine of these are in the North East, including North Ormesby).

Even areas lucky enough to be picked out for such investment face an uphill challenge, considering the mix of social challenges they face. Others, more so. Even with substantial investment, deprived neighbourhoods tend to stay deprived. Now that investment is unlikely to come. Whether it does or not, neighbourhoods are being obliged to look to their internal resources to negotiate challenge and change.

> **Even with substantial investment, deprived neighbourhoods tend to stay deprived. Now that investment is unlikely to come. Whether it does or not, neighbourhoods are being obliged to look to their internal resources to negotiate challenge and change.**

This is the case for resilience.

Defining resilience

Resilience, not unlike 'community', is a 'purr word', almost guaranteed to excite a positive response. Who would say that resilience is a bad thing? It is synonymous with hardiness, positivity, and pluckiness, and a refusal to bow in the face of adverse circumstance. In fact, 'communities' are often commended for their 'resilience' after terrible events. The problem with this loose understanding is that it can be attached to any 'community', in any acute or long-term difficulty, with the sole qualification being that the subject is 'getting on' with life, as if there were a choice.

66

> ## Who would say that resilience is a bad thing? It is synonymous with hardiness, positivity, and pluckiness, and a refusal to bow in the face of adverse circumstance.

To be resilient is to have the ability to 'snap' or 'bounce' back from the effects of external pressure. Andrew Zolli and Ann Marie Healy's popular book, *Resilience: Why Things Bounce Back* tellingly has a cover image of a bundle of elastic bands.[14] The implication is that the most basic sense of the word is enough: the Latin *resilire*, meaning to rebound or recoil. It is a metaphor drawn from material science: "the ability of a material to absorb energy when it is deformed elastically, and release that energy upon unloading".

If this is what it means, then resilience would have no real significance for description or analysis. We are far from the first people to suggest that an equivalence between the physical and social or psychological, emotional or spiritual meanings of resilience is a mistake. It is too simplistic to capture social and relational dynamics, and would not include any aspect of human meaning-making. If resilience is to mean anything in the social world, it needs to be able to incorporate both endurance and adaption, growth, learning – perhaps evening strengthening.

Better analogies spring from the ideas around ecological resilience. An ecology might only experience a certain amount of eternal pressure before reaching a 'threshold' and 'catastrophic regime shift'. After such a shift, an ecology can achieve a stable state after change or trauma but it will be different from the one before. Applied to the social world, this helpfully reminds us that resilience can result from complex independent factors, that it can be unpredictable, and that it is limited. In itself, however, this isn't entirely satisfactory. An ecology system has no agency, and human agency is an important part of neighbourhood resilience.

There is also a fear that talk of resilience can be inversely correlated to the amount of help that a neighbourhood might receive. During interviews and conversations around this project, we often encountered a concern that resilience is about shifting the burden of the delivery of public justice away from public authorities and onto individuals and communities. Resilience is a kind of 'damned if you do and damned if you don't' scenario: non-resilient communities are held culpable for their own struggles, while resilient communities are assumed to have the capacity to fend for themselves.

A more scholarly version of this complaint is put by Jonathan Joseph in his paper, 'Resilience as embedded neoliberalism: a governmentality approach'.

During interviews and conversations around this project, we often encountered a concern that resilience is about shifting the burden of the delivery of public justice away from public authorities and onto individuals and communities.

> In the process of constructing and interpellating neoliberal subjects, neoliberal discourse and practices appeal to them as citizens or consumers who are 'free' to take responsibility for their own life choices, but who are expected to follow competitive rules of conduct. Governmentality works by telling us to be enterprising, active and responsible citizens. Neoliberalism works through the social production of freedom and the 'management and organization of the conditions in which one can be free'.
>
> Resilience contributes to this through its stress on heightened self-awareness, reflexivity and responsibility. It encourages the idea of active citizenship, whereby people, rather than relying on the state, take responsibility for their own social and economic well-being...[15]

For critics like Joseph the point of resilience is not for communities to develop agency to overcome change and challenge where the state is unable to act, but to discipline different parts of the state. He also notes that in many cases community empowerment is actually government from a distance (i.e., communities are told that that must be empowered even if they have no desire to take on greater responsibility for welfare etc).

This is a powerful critique, and one primarily rooted in ethical and ideological concerns which will be broadly shared. There are both ethical and practical rejoinders. Yes, to a degree people must (and can) take responsibility for their own social and economic well-being. Crucially, however, that 'taking of responsibility' is not an individual but collective act. It is not as if there is nothing between the state and the individual. Indeed, it is intermediary association which humanises what Joseph calls neoliberalism.

That said, as we observe above, Joseph is right to say that the push for resilience comes from high level policy change which effectively sees some communities as too far gone to bother with, and the rest to be assisted mainly by economic development. The practical rejoinder is that yes – the turn to resilience is partly necessitated by changes in political approach, but that does not mean that it can or should be avoided. Alongside efforts to see re-investment in neighbourhoods, neighbourhoods should look to understand how they can build resilience.

> **Alongside efforts to see re-investment in neighbourhoods, neighbourhoods should look to understand how they can build resilience.**

People, place and purpose

There is no obvious or simple definition of the concept of neighbourhood, though it is more meaningful than synonyms such as 'community'. The word holds a tension between geographical and social meaning. At one end of this spectrum there lies the ward or, for statistical purposes, 'lower super output area'. At the other end sits self- and collectively-defined space – the neighbourhood in people's perception.[16] Neighbourhood is therefore less of a technical concept than the lived space, which may or may not match geographical boundaries like wards or parishes.[17]

All neighbourhoods have a social ecology of facilities and services – libraries, schools, health centres, parks etc. – alongside community institutions, relationships and spaces that make a neighbourhood a neighbourhood. It is the ways that people inhabit a particular place and make sense together of their lives there.

This social ecology is concrete and tangible, including things like community centres, but it also has intangible aspects. We could call this the 'spirit' – indeed, the spirituality – of an area. What stories are told about a neighbourhood – are they pessimistic or optimistic? Who is telling them and what values do they communicate, implicitly or explicitly? What sense of identity does it have?

What makes a social ecology resilient? Researchers have listed a variety of factors thought to contribute. This includes the presence of active citizens within the community – people who possess the skills to lead local initiatives and encourage other community members to participate.[18] 'Deprived' communities can be short on residents with the confidence and tacit skills that facilitate leadership. The presence of healthy numbers of volunteers is another significant resilience indicator,[19] as is a physical environment that engenders pride in the community and a shared sense of belonging.[20] Researchers also point to good relations between community members and the local authorities, and state that "community festivals and events [can] promote social mixing and pride in the area [but they] often rely on the support and input of council workers" that is, these events are often joint efforts.[21] At the core, relationships are often highlighted as central in the formation of community resilience – people working together, helping each other, and co-ordinating with

Relationships are often highlighted as central in the formation of community resilience – people working together, helping each other, and co-ordinating with other organisations in the area to ensure that the needs of the community are met where possible.

other organisations in the area to ensure that the needs of the community are met where possible.[22]

By distilling these various indicators of resilience, and by drawing lessons from our case study neighbourhoods, we are drawn to three domains/themes underlying neighbourhood resilience. These are people, place and purpose – or, more technically, social capital, physical capital and spiritual capital.

— Social capital is a familiar term, and one contested in its own right. At its most basic, however, it points to the importance and value of social networks for effective action – the habits of trust, reciprocity and commonality that allow individuals and institutions to operate together. Both 'bonding' and 'bridging' capital are significant for understanding resilience, and the development of local leadership is a significant aspect of the building and social capital.

— Physical capital is easier to grasp – it consists of buildings, facilities and spaces of public gathering (the more traditional meaning of social infrastructure). Multiple questions occur. First, are there any? Second, are there enough? Third, how are they 'enacted' as public spaces – are they used inclusively, in ways that create connections between different parts of a community?

— Spiritual capital is not a familiar term, though neither is it new. Matthew Guest has used the term to describe "the flow of [spiritual] influences and resources acquired through the life course" of an individual.[23] Others have used it as a theoretical framework through which to understand the relationship between spiritual practices and economic life. We use it here to describe the way that churches (and others) shape local identities and offer symbolic moments of celebration or mourning. We are using it here to draw attention to intangible factors which contribute to a sense of hope or conversely to a sense of despair. In resilience literature, this perhaps most closely correlates with discussion of local identities.

Churches and resilience

It is widely recognised that churches have reserves of social capital. They are, of course, effectively membership organisations that integrate a worshipping life, 'internal' community and social and public purpose. Nick Spencer has described this as "Christian social liturgy".[24] In Robert Putnam's phrase, religion can have the effect of bringing "moral freighting" to relationships, meaning that religiosity is a good predictor of volunteering, charitable giving, and other forms of public action. Of course, the reserve of social capital is not endless: particularly, church congregations are growing older, and the 'bridging' between different institutions is not always trouble-free. We will consider this in greater depth in the next chapter.

We also know that churches have physical capital that can be used for the benefit of the wider community. It has been observed that churches are often the only non-commercial public spaces left in deprived communities, and can be important spaces of hospitality and help in difficult times – see, for instance, Amy Plender's recent report on faith-based responses to the Grenfell tragedy.[25] Again, our argument

> **It has been observed that churches are often the only non-commercial public spaces left in deprived communities, and can be important spaces of hospitality and help in difficult times.**

isn't that churches own and control public space – in fact, the more interesting question is what happens when they don't, or their spaces are difficult to use. We will consider this in greater depth in chapter 3.

Spiritual capital, as we have said, is a far less familiar term. In our case studies, however, it was striking how meaning is found in an area's past, present and future – shared stories about what life 'round here' is like. Of course, there was not always consensus – quite the opposite, in fact. People involved in neighbourhood action were often consciously narrating *against* other stories – such as that compared to a past 'golden age' the present was bleak and hopeless. Even the names given to projects were consciously freighted.

Meaning is found in an area's past, present and future – shared stories about what life 'round here' is like.

> *These community relationships were developing just as austerity began to bite and people started to talk about the need to do something. 'Shildon Alive' became that 'something' with the name reflecting our belief in abundant life for all.*[26]

It is common knowledge that churches contribute much in terms of compassionate action – e.g., food banks, debt advice, welfare advocacy services, youthwork, food poverty/ food waste reduction, credit union activities, memory cafés and community gardening activities. However, churches' contribution to resilience rests on something other than, and goes beyond, 'social action'.

Our empirical case studies found resonances across each of these themes. We also found dissonances and limitations in each domain – ways in which churches were failing to connect their resilience to the wider community. Rather than proceeding by giving some form of scorecard for each neighbourhood/church, we will address each of these subthemes in turn, before at the conclusion of each chapter drawing attention to areas where there seem to be gaps.

Our overall contention is that many churches will have deposits of each of these forms of social capital – people, place and purpose. If they can make these assets available to others, they are well placed to help build neighbourhood resilience.

1 Chris Tighe, 'Redcar struggles to recover one year after steel plant closure', *Financial Times*, 12 October 2016. www.ft.com/content/8c02c6b2-8e77-11e6-8df8-d3778b55a923

2 David Ford, *The Shape of Living: Spiritual Directions for Everyday Life*. (Norwich: Canterbury Press, 2012). Ann Morisy used the concept of "multiple overwhelmings" at our 'Faith in Troubled Times' conference in Newcastle in October of 2017 (unpublished talk).

3 North East Local Economic Partnership, *Our Economy 2018*. www.nelep.co.uk/oureconomy/

4 Luke Raikes, 'State of the North 2017: The Millennial Powerhouse', *IPPR North* (November 2017) p. 18.

5 Andrew Hood and Tom Waters, 'Living standards, poverty and inequality in the UK: 2017-18 to 2021-22' *Institute for Fiscal Studies* (2017). www.ifs.org.uk/publications/10028

6 That said, on 'contextual value added' assessments (that is, taking account of the variety of factors which may adversely affect pupil attainment) schools in the North East are amongst the best in the country – in spite of the fact that funding for non-London schools is generally lower. See Jonathon Clifton, Anna Round and Luke Raikes, 'Northern Schools: putting education at the heart of the northern powerhouse', *IPPR North* (May 2016).

7 Nationally only five local authority areas in the UK are predicted to experience a proportional growth in under-65s.

8 OADR is defined as the proportion of people of State Pension age relative to the working age population, expressed as the proportion of dependants per 1,000 working age population.

9 House of Commons Home Affairs Committee, *Asylum Accommodation*, Twelfth Report of Session 2016–17 p. 16. publications.parliament.uk/pa/cm201617/cmselect/cmhaff/637/637.pdf

10 Matthew Ward, 'Statistics on UK-EU trade', *House of Commons Briefing Paper 7851*, 1 May 2018 researchbriefings.files.parliament.uk/documents/CBP-7851/CBP-7851.pdf

11 Department for Communities and Local Government, *Estate Regeneration National Strategy: case studies*, 2016, assets.publishing.service.gov.uk/government/uploads/system/uploads/attachment_data/file/575764/Estate_regeneration_case_studies.pdf

12 Ed Cox et al, 'Love thy Neighbourhood: People and Place in Social Reform', *IPPR North* (2013), p. 40.

13 Alasdair Rae, Ruth Hamilton, Rich Crisp and Ryan Powell, *Overcoming deprivation and disconnection in UK cities*, (JRF, 2016), p. 10.

14 Andrew Zolli and Ann Marie Healy, *Resilience: Why Things Bounce Back*, (London: Hatchett, 2012).

15 Jonathan Joseph, 'Resilience as embedded neoliberalism: a governmentality approach', *Resilience*, 1:1, (2013) pp. 38-52, DOI: 10.1080/21693293.2013.765741

16 The Young Foundation, *How can neighbourhoods be understood and defined?* 2010, youngfoundation.org/wp-content/uploads/2012/11/How-can-neighbourhoods-be-understood-and-defined-August-2010.pdf

17 See a helpful discussion in Cox et al, 'Love thy Neighbourhood' (2013) p. 1.

18 Deborah Platts-Fowler and David Robinson, *Neighbourhood Resilience in Sheffield: Getting By in Hard Times*, (Sheffield, Sheffield Hallam University, 2013), p. 22;

19 Ibid., p. 18.

20 Ibid., p. 20.

21 Ibid., p. 21.

22 Steve Cinderby, Dr Gary Haq, Howard Cambridge and Kate Lock, *Practical action to build community resilience: The Good Life initiative in New Earswick*, (Joseph Rowntree Foundation, 2014), p.4.

23 Matthew Guest, 'In search of spiritual capital: the spiritual as a cultural resource', in *The Sociology of Spirituality* (Aldershot: Ashgate, 2007), pp. 181-200.

24 Nick Spencer, *Doing Good: A Future for Christianity in the 21st Century* (Theos, 2016), p. 12.

25 Amy Plender, *After Grenfell: the Faith Groups' Response* (Theos, 2018).

26 See shildonalive.org.uk/

2
People

CHAPTER 2 SUMMARY

— Social capital describes the levels of trust, reciprocity and cooperative action in a community. The chapter draws out three aspects: how individuals benefit, volunteering and activism, and cooperation between institutional leaders.

— Supporting individuals in appropriate ways – building their resilience – contributes to neighbourhood resilience in the long run.

— Levels of volunteering in case study areas were mixed, but churches were engaging diverse groups across racial and religious divides.

— There was a diversity of community organisations in each case study neighbourhood with varying levels of collaboration. The small and fragmented nature of grassroots community work is seen as a problem, but can be overcome.

Social capital is about the value of social networks, bonding similar people and bridging between diverse people, with norms of reciprocity.[1] The term has been endlessly differentiated: bonding, bridging, linking, structural, cognitive and so on. At its core, it is fundamentally about how people interact with each other.[2] Do people know and trust each other? Do they feel at home? Are there people who can help them? Beyond this, do they get involved in local networks, through either membership or volunteering? Do they have a sense of agency and control over their own lives?

Scholars connect resilience and social capital in a variety of ways. First, networks of friendship and trust are seen as vital for the resilience of individuals – relationships are seen as a social resource on which individuals can draw in difficult times. Second, high levels of volunteering and activism are synonymous with high levels of social capital – resilience literature also points to the presence of key 'super-volunteers', activists or connectors. Third, 'bridging' social capital describes collaboration between difference agencies or institutions. This supports 'collective efficacy' – that is, the ability to achieve things together where they can't easily be achieved by a single institution or actor.

We'll examine how churches support each of these in turn, before concluding the chapter by identifying areas where there might be opportunity for more focused and deliberate action.

An individual perspective

This is my home. I've never had a home. Since I was 16 this is the longest place that I've been settled somewhere. [I] generally move every six months... I've never felt welcome anywhere. I find it peaceful, so friendly, the people here, there's such a community and everyone wants to help everyone and that makes me want to stay here. This is my home now. I ain't moving nowhere else.

Project volunteer, Case Study A

All three of our case study neighbourhoods are areas of relatively high deprivation. In the latest Index of Multiple Deprivation (IMD) Shildon East ward ranked 544, Byker was ranked 403 out of 32,844 in England. North Ormesby ranks at 2. In short, these are some of the most deprived neighbourhoods in the country, each facing their own unique mix of social and economic challenges. Ultimately, the rankings are expressed in poverty and isolation.

On one of our case visits, I met Ted (not his real name). Ted told me that he had struggled at school – his behaviour wasn't great. He left as soon as he could, and got shift work in a local factory. It was physically demanding and he didn't last long. There was a few years' stability with a window cleaning job, but a bout of ill health meant he had to quit. It wasn't long before things got bad. Pride kept him away from the Foodbank – "I knew people would see me" – until, "in the end I had no choice". I asked Ted if he had friends or family nearby. "Yes – my brother, but I couldn't go to him for help. We don't get on."

Despite his initial reticence, the Foodbank has been a big help for Ted. It was the first step into a network of relationships and support that met his immediate physical need for food and then offered longer-term support. The project had recently provided him with a small loan so he could move to other accommodation. The last place, he said, had been riddled with damp and other problems ("the landlord didn't give a toss"), but Ted had been trapped there because he couldn't get a bond together.

While I was talking to him one of the project workers stuck her head through the door. Could he lock up, she asked, jangling a heavy bunch of keys at him. I was a little surprised – was Ted a client or a trusted volunteer? He couldn't help on that occasion – he had a 2 o'clock at the job centre.

Ted's is not an atypical story, of course. The low-pay no-pay cycle made his life a precarious one. Illness pushed over the house of cards. Building individual resilience is one way of articulating what seems to be the very heart of Christian social action – simple one-to-one encounters where someone arrives with a complex set of problems and issues. They may take years to unravel but they begin with friendship, and friendship is one of the things that makes the difference.

> *One of the biggest things I feel about our position in the community is that people are in need of friendship, someone to talk to, they know that coming here the friendship is here, they can talk to us knowing that we will listen and if we can we will help. They know they have friends here.*
>
> **Church member, Case Study C**

Of course, many people don't know – Ted didn't, and desperation for a meal was the thing that took him along. What was interesting about him was that it didn't stop with friendship. "What would you like to be doing in the future?" I asked. "Stuff like this," he said, signalling at the shelves half-full of canned goods. He wanted to help others. His own resilience was developing, and now he saw ways he could contribute.

This departure into an individual's resilience isn't a step back from the wider conversation about what it is for neighbourhoods to flourish. Ted's newfound stability was turning this recipient of help into a provider and collaborator. Not that he saw himself as a church member.

All the churches we visited had adopted the language of 'with, not for or to'. In Ted's case – and in others – this had worked. It was by no means a simple task to build people's sense of agency, and then to see that agency appropriately deployed and supported.

This leads us to the second element – levels of volunteering and social activism.

Levels of volunteering and activism

It is hotly debated whether religiosity leads to higher levels of volunteering. Robert Putnam's findings in *American Grace* have not been so clearly repeated elsewhere. For instance, one recent analysis of the European Values Study observes that religious volunteers are more likely to volunteer for associations of their own religion, but not for others.[3]

Of course it is impossible to adjudicate on that on the basis of three case studies, no matter how immersive. What emerges is more interesting, however.

First, one case study had managed to build a large and thriving network of volunteers, so many that they had been forced to run a fairly strict shift system to make sure there weren't too many in their small community space at one time. We attended a project impact session. There were perhaps 20 volunteers in the room engaged in helping on quite an array of projects, from community gardening to a memory café. We were told there could have been more had it not been for a concentration of similar meetings in the calendar. It was clear that collectively, the volunteers were highly motivated, engaged and trained. "They seem to have kept their volunteers which is really good, and they've become more sophisticated volunteers, more skills and training under their belt," said one leader of a partner organisation. It was also clear that they were by no means all church members. There was therefore a double benefit – not only were services provided and needs met, but the very fact

> One recent analysis of the European Values Study observes that religious volunteers are more likely to volunteer for associations of their own religion, but not for others.

that local volunteers were delivering the project saw them empowered. The church leader said, "What we're doing will have lasting impact because it's done by local people".

The other two case study neighbourhoods felt different. One in particular identified a lack of volunteers as a key weakness in their ministry. Leaders and staff felt that the wider church were not as willing to volunteer for various community sessions as they could be. The burden fell largely on clergy and a small staff team.

Interviewees also reported concern about an ageing activist base, and were consciously trying to engage another generation. This was meeting with some success, including with those who were relatively new to church. In a similar way to Ted, they were on a journey of increasing confidence and engagement, though starting at a different place.

At some point, people lending a hand on this or that project is not enough. Organisers are required – and this often depends on greater confidence, more training, and more education. These are often the very things that are lacking in areas of high deprivation.

> *I was nominated for church warden two years ago. [The vicar] said, "I want you to pray about it". I just laughed at him! But it's improved my confidence and made me learn more about church not just being on a Sunday... I've learnt to grow up a lot.*
>
> **Church volunteer, Case Study C**

This moves to a question not just of agency, or volunteering, but ultimately one of 'leadership' – and not in the clerical or religious sense. At some point, people lending a hand on this or that project is not enough. Organisers are required – and this often depends on greater confidence, more training, and more education. These are often the very things that are lacking in areas of high deprivation. Talented leadership healthily reproduces itself. A community project manager in one of our case study neighbourhoods spoke about how her confidence and skills had been built.

> I'm not insular, I don't do everything myself. I give people the skills and trust them, telling them they can do it. I couldn't work out why they gave me a section of the grant form to fill out... It was hard but I did it. Giving someone a new challenge, giving them the skills and then the challenge – that's another element of community development.
>
> **Project manager, Case Study A**

This is complex work. It can also challenge assumptions about what 'religious' volunteering looks like. The binary categories of bridging and bonding didn't seem to map easily onto this situation. The projects, whether run directly by the church or by charities established by the church, were 'faith-based', but serving without discrimination, and indeed inviting those of other faiths or none into the heart of what the church was seeking to do.

> A lot of the people volunteering in our youth and children's work are Muslim, and some Hindu. One or two of them are taking a leading role in that. We're in the strange situation of being a Christian church where some of the people in leadership are not only not Christians, but active members of other faiths. That's an interesting dynamic. At the same time, we have some people who are making the journey from Islam to Christianity. So actually, there's a very complex...

Interviewer – And you want to encourage them without making it feel like a hostile environment for...?

Exactly. We have to honour those of the Muslim faith. At the same time as there still being that invitation to explore Christianity but not in a way that feels at all cajoling or manipulative.

Church leader, Case Study C

The point then is that the boundary between the social capital of the church and the social capital of the wider community is fuzzy. Churches and church-based projects are not only for the religious. They often aren't even being delivered by religious volunteers. Volunteer-based organisations are as much about the volunteers as those they 'serve'. Developmental, relational work with people to find and build their gifting is as important as the rest of the activity.

Cooperation across institutions

As we have said, the case study neighbourhoods are among the most deprived in the country. One of the things that indicates that they are nevertheless resilient is the diversity of faith-based and non faith-based organisations intent on improving the area and serving residents.

The boundary between the social capital of the church and the social capital of the wider community is fuzzy.

Two of our case study areas had the church as part of a dense collaborative network of organisations and institutions. Those networks comprised public sector/civic officials, local schools, community development groups, BME groups, other churches and religious organisations and housing associations. This diversity of organisations was celebrated.

> *There's a lot of positive stuff going on and I think that can sometimes be [overlooked] and people focus on negative things, but I have to say [this project] is probably one of the best community spirit places I've been to and worked within. The town I'm from is nothing like this. It's wealthier but they're missing the community aspects.*

Church staff member, Case Study A

In two of the three case studies, there were numerous examples of practical collaboration. In one case, this was partly driven by the Big Local programme (which the church leader had been invited to chair). Among other things that the programme had supported was extended youth work, run by the church but funded by the Big Local grant – described to me as the most highly regarded in the area – a 'community face-lift', and the development of a Community Land Trust. In the other case study, collaboration was less formal but still very substantial, particularly with local schools.

Church leaders tended to function as the main connectors or collaborators. With almost no reservations, they were highly regarded.

> *The biggest relationship we have locally is with [X] church and that's around [the minister] building that relationship. He's very, very proactive, you know "let's not talk about it, let's get on with it." ... Sometimes the small things help – it's not necessarily throwing money at things, just bringing the right people together. He's the one that's come in and started this process... The church is out in the community now...we don't view it as the*

*church but we all work together so we more and more think of
the church as accessible.*

Local government officer, Case Study A

Meaningful collaboration is not always easy – either
between the church and other institutions or indeed other
institutions and each other. This was simply a matter of trust;
very often an organisation was perceived as having a particular
vested or hidden interest.

This, bluntly, was often a matter of money. Either different
institutions were competing against each other to be seen as
the people 'doing the stuff' in a neighbourhood, and hence
the most worthy of financial support, or they had some
commercial interest (e.g., housing associations who were only
about supporting tenants in their
own properties: "they promise so
much, and they never really deliver
on things... It's still cash in the
register").

**Meaningful collaboration
is not always easy – either
between the church and
other institutions or indeed
other institutions and
each other.**

Churches (usually) didn't have
to persuade people that they didn't
want to control all the money,
though they occasionally had to
overcome latent fears about religion.
In one case, the relationship between
a church and a community centre had taken a turn for the
worse some years previously with a conflict over the water
supply, and had only recently been restored.

However, there had been times and places where conflict
was necessary. Indeed, certain kinds of conflict are an
expression of resilience. One interviewee spoke to us about

having to be "a thorn in the side" of statutory agencies that didn't necessarily understand the community "from the inside".

> *... they come up with a plan of how to improve us but it wouldn't ever work because no one lives their lives like that. It's got to make sense to the way people are living their lives, at a time and place and offering something relevant.*

Church leader, Case Study C

Are there areas here where the churches could further support resilience? We believe there are.

Gaps

There is ample evidence above that churches are building reserves of social capital, supporting individuals, providing creative and surprising ways for people to serve in their community, and collaborating with others in supporting change. Are there areas here where the churches could further support resilience? We believe there are.

Supporting individuals

Churches clearly have an ongoing role in relational social action – the business of simply meeting the needs of individuals. Those now seem to be as much about loneliness and local connection as they are about simple material needs.

> *I used to like popping for a little chat because I'm on my own most of the time. It's all gone by the by these last few months. I'd love to get back into it because I feel like I don't belong to anywhere now. I've got a sense of belonging from being here.*

Community member, Case Study B

However, one key insight from the perspective of resilience is that some kinds of compassionate action can undermine individual or community well-being in the long term.[4] There was a recognition that some interventions – particularly food distribution without thoughtful follow-up – were probably irresponsible.

> *We want to be a church with people rather than for people... One of the issues this community has is the fact that in estates like this people are quite used to going to people for things - not necessarily that they're lazy or don't do things for themselves. But I think the church could be perceived like any other agency or institution where you come for a service and have an expectation of what the church should be doing. We've been thinking about how that isn't a sustainable thing for us here. We have to work out how to be with people.*

Church leader, Case Study B

In practice, there were some activities giving people free food or clothes. Once it's started, that kind of thing is difficult to stop. One project worker spoke of the difficulty of negotiating healthy relational boundaries, particularly with people who arrived with mental health needs.

> *She Face-Timed me the other evening, I didn't answer because I've got children. We were watching a film etc. I said I didn't answer because I assumed she'd done it by accident, but she'd rang to prove to someone who I was. That I was her friend... Most people understand that we go home at night to our families. But then when mental health and other issues come into play they don't understand relationships.*

Project manager, Case Study A

Some groups were making an effort to shift the culture, particularly around food poverty. Foodbanks and community supermarkets became projects to minimise food waste, often including a small charge or membership fee. In some cases this genuinely seemed to change patterns of use, drawing custom from a more diverse mix of people and giving people a sense that they were contributing to a social good (which indeed, they were). In other cases, it didn't seem that the change of name/approach had had the desired effect.

Volunteering and activism

As we have said, encouraging volunteering and activism is crucial for resilience. The case study neighbourhoods did feel like they were experiencing different levels of engagement. While in all areas there was a strong network of community organisations, in at least one case it seemed as if the balance of the work was being done by paid employees.

In one case – ironically the one where the church project has done best at recruiting, training and retaining volunteers – there was a marked absence of male volunteers. We asked the minister why he thought this was the case.

> *There are positives but these surround the strength of the women who have held things together despite everything. All the key organisations in the town are now run by women. They know what they need to do to create community and they do it with one another really well. It's more marked now they don't have strong men alongside them. All the women in the hub who are married, their husbands suffer from mental illness.*

Church leader, Case Study A

This highlights the need to be attentive to local factors when seeking to build resilience, and potential 'cold spots' in terms of any social capital that can be built. For instance, a relatively small proportion of the leaders we encountered in any institution – sacred or secular – originated from the immediate neighbourhood, a result perhaps of the relative lack of volunteering and activism in deprived communities?

A relatively small proportion of the leaders we encountered in any institution – sacred or secular – originated from the immediate neighbourhood.

> *Back then all the doctors lived in the town, professional classes. A road here [was] nicknamed "nobs' row" because that's where the bosses used to live. Now it's absentee landlords, falling into disrepair... People who have that skilled background, confidence, don't live here, so we don't have the kind of skill set that maybe a more middle class town would have to do things and run things. Even in the church a lot of our folk are fairly wounded people, I don't know where we'll get a church treasurer from in the future, those sorts of roles, because the skill sets aren't here.*

Church leader, Case Study A

There is clearly more work for churches – and others – to do if they want to build agency in these neighbourhoods.

Collaboration

We have highlighted the high levels of collaboration between different institutions and groups, and indeed some of the difficulties. We have also said that church leaders were almost universally well-regarded by community stakeholders. There is a challenge, however, to move beyond warm relationships to tangible and purposeful collaboration. In areas that have benefited from Big Local the issue is forced. In other contexts, there was a concern that community action in deprived neighbourhoods was simply too fragmentary.

66

There is a challenge, however, to move beyond warm relationships to tangible and purposeful collaboration.

The way that funding and stuff is going at the moment is that there'll be a targeted youth provision that will go out to tender. It relies on consortia... It seems to me that there are quite a lot of good, [well-intentioned] people trying to do things, but it's kind of in a small grassroots sort of a way. If we don't pull together and form some sort of [consortium] then the funding will end up going to big organisations who don't know the local area like we all do. It's clear to me that unless people work in a really collaborative way then they won't get funded.

Housing Association officer, Case Study B

Sometimes, community organisations simply 'cohabit' in a neighbourhood without collaborating, though not through a shortage of good will. Funders can take measures to try to encourage greater inter-agency work, but the problem is an adaptive rather than a technical one. In other words, it requires learning, probably by exposure to good models of co-operation (i.e., models of genuine partnership, rather than where community organisations are simply delivery mechanisms for goals set elsewhere).

Finally, there was one obvious gap in these networks of collaboration. Churches were present, schools were present, elected politicians were part of the conversation, local government officers were too. Community centres and housing associations were part of the network. However, in none of the case study areas were local businesses or employers engaged in any systematic way – if anything, businesses were occasionally approached for donations. Businesses will have different goals than community organisations and churches, but that doesn't mean that they don't have a stake in the social ecology. Many business leaders readily accept this, and may be willing to support local charities with time and expertise as well as donations. One of the uses of social capital is connecting individuals to opportunities for work. Better connections with local businesses could lift aspirations. Businesses might want to support community development work. This would be an area for further exploration.

1   Paul Dekker and Eric M Uslaner, *Social Capital and Participation in Everyday Life* (London: Routledge, 2001), pp. 1-8.

2   Dekker and Uslaner, *Social Capital and Participation* (2001) p. 7.

3   Ingrid Storm, 'Civic Engagement in Britain: The Role of Religion and Inclusive Values', *European Sociological Review* (2015), Vol. 31, No. 1, pp. 14–29.

4   See for instance Robert D Lupton, *Toxic Charity: How the Church Hurts Those They Help and How to Reverse It* (New York: Harper Collins, 2011). Lupton distinguishes between crisis intervention and community development, arguing that churches tend to prefer the former.

3
Place

CHAPTER 3 SUMMARY

— Physical and public spaces of gathering are important for neighbourhood resilience. There is concern that many areas now lack such spaces.

— Some churches have multi-purpose community buildings, the importance of which is hard to overestimate, particularly as other spaces of gathering (pubs, community centres, youth clubs) are closing. Ensuring communities have such spaces is a key future priority.

— Other churches have spaces that don't readily lend themselves to community service or community development purposes. Churches operate out of improvised shop front spaces, often hampered by their size and lack of versatility.

— Simply having space that is open to the community is not enough. If they are not properly used they can fail to be places of genuine mixing.

Community facilities, buildings, spaces of gathering, physical and social infrastructure – what we call physical capital – are vital for supporting neighbourhood resilience. It's not just what you do that counts, but the fact that you have somewhere to do it – indeed, the former relies on the latter. In a recent Theos report on faith groups' response to the Grenfell fire, Amy Plender observes a "practical explanation for the efficacy of the faith groups' response, namely the available space in their buildings".[1]

In a recent essay for the Local Trust, Dan Gregory calls the scale of loss of community space "terrifying": 28,000 pubs since the 1970s, 121 libraries closed in 2016, 600 youth centres closed between 2012 and 2016, 1,200 children's centres have shut since 2010.[2] His list goes on and on, noting also that 110 Anglican churches have been closed in Wales in the last ten years.

Religious buildings are not just places of worship (in the narrow sense). They are also often iconic buildings that shape local identity, places of public gathering and integration, and places of public action. Paradoxically they can be hugely burdensome. Sometimes, the best thing that can happen to a church is that one of their buildings burns down or falls down. The congregation will mourn what is lost, but will be relieved of the all-absorbing task of preventing the roof from leaking. It will also have the opportunity to reimagine its mission in a way not tied to what are often Victorian – or older – facilities. What might a neighbourhood need for the next hundred years, as opposed to the last?

Given the frightening rate at which public spaces and facilities – including green spaces – are being lost, one of the key contributions churches can make to neighbourhood resilience is a public space. Simply having buildings is not enough, however; they have to be 'enacted' in the right way.

In this chapter, we will first reflect on what buildings and spaces were available in the case study neighbourhoods as a whole and with the churches specifically. We will then consider their use.

One of the key contributions churches can make to neighbourhood resilience is a public space. Simply having buildings is not enough, however; they have to be 'enacted' in the right way.

Each of our three case study areas confirm the argument that there is a decreasing amount of community space available.

North Ormesby

In North Ormesby there are two important community spaces.

One is the council-run 'community hub' – the base for rationalised council services after the local library and youth centre closed down. The hub contains a smaller library, rooms for training and a free computer suite, a dance studio and boxing club, and a day nursery. Youth clubs were hosted there, though they were run by the church youth project and funded through Big Local. They were drawing around 40 children twice-weekly. The centre manager told us that she was part of a team of five people overseeing all the 'hub' facilities in Middlesbrough. There had been 11 people in the team. Most of the community hubs were heavily volunteer-driven.

The other is the Trinity Centre. By the late 1990s, the old church hall had been demolished and after extensive fundraising was rebuilt as a multipurpose facility. The adjoining church building has an interesting history in its own right. After a fire in 1977, the church was rebuilt with a smaller worshipping space, and the chancel retained as a cloister, which now sits between the church and the centre and is accessible from both. This creates a peaceful and pleasant outdoor space – something which North Ormesby otherwise lacks. The building's development was cited in Middlesbrough Council's regeneration documents as the catalyst to the development of North Ormesby Health Village in 2008 and the redevelopment of the housing surrounding the church between 2008 and 2010, and finally the market place in 2011.[3]

Byker

In comparison, Byker lacks community spaces – or at least it lacks them where they are needed. Most facilities are toward the north of the neighbourhood, on the Shields Road or just to the south of Byker Wall. These include St Michael's Church and the Byker Community Centre – both substantial, though old, buildings. The community centre was originally the church hall. At some point, it was sold to Newcastle Council, and then passed from the Newcastle Council to Byker Community Association through Community Asset Transfer. The centre has a large function room used by multiple groups throughout the week. It also hosts a pay-as-you-feel supermarket.[4]

The church is a large Victorian building, set in grounds with impressive views over Newcastle. This green space was redeveloped in 2011 with a Big Lottery/Groundwork grant of £450,000, creating an amphitheatre and community allotment. This outdoor space is still pleasant but has signs of wear and tear (and abuse – there are not irregular instances of vandalism in the outdoor space and on the church itself). The building itself is used mainly for the church's Sunday worship, though this is within a marquee erected inside the building to keep down heating costs.

The church had been meeting in their shop front space – the Cross Café (named after its immediate location, Raby Cross) until relatively recently. That space is now in frequent use during the week, and sits near a collection of Byker's community organisations. These include the Byker Community Trust, ACANE (African Community Advice North East) and Life Vineyard Church (which runs a membership-based food project – the Byker Pantry).

Shildon

As a small town in its own right, as opposed to urban villages within a larger metropolitan whole, Shildon has a different feel. Most of the community spaces are based on Church Street, the town's main street.

Livin Housing – a housing association managing around 8,400 homes across County Durham – operates 'Foundations', a project which inhabits a slightly-larger than shop front space with meeting rooms, kitchens, and offices. This is supported by the Sunderland Football Club's Foundation of Light, Health Express and Durham County Council. A short walk up the road brings you to Shildon Alive's hub – in a previous life this was a small two-up, two-down home. Downstairs is a small seating area with computers, a coffee machine, and fresh food to take on a pay-as-you-feel basis. Behind this, there's a very small office space, variously the home of the benefits advocacy worker, financial literacy worker and credit union volunteer. Upstairs the project manager has a tiny desk in a room crowded with shelving for foodstuffs and other donations.

Further down the road is a health centre, closed since the surgery occupying the building merged with another elsewhere in the town. Across from this stands St John's Church, built in 1834 and then extended in the latter part of the nineteenth century. It is a well-maintained building, and includes a mezzanine that is used for meetings and toddler and youth groups.

Around the corner is Shildon Methodist Church, which maintains a small hall. In the south of the town there is a large Salvation Army church and centre, and to the south east the Jubilee Fields Community Centre.

Enacted places

In each of these neighbourhoods it was clear the physical environment – including community facilities and green spaces – was an important part of the 'social ecology'. The mere presence of buildings, however, isn't in the point. Their significance for resilience only emerges by understanding this dynamic combination of the spaces themselves and the things that happen in them – the way that they are 'enacted'.[5]

The Trinity Centre in North Ormesby is in some ways a case apart, and not just because of its relative size, or the way the church tower can be seen from much of east Middlesbrough. It is also run as a Community Interest Company. Surplus income generated from conference facilities is reinvested into the church's various community projects. The Centre has the advantage of a large amount of parking outside on the market square, making it a convenient conference space, and a Tuesday market brings a large amount of footfall into the café. The Trinity Youth and Children's Project – a separate charity within a family of Holy Trinity North Ormesby projects and activities – is also housed in the building.

The roles of the Trinity Centre and the Community Hub also seemed helpfully defined. The Community Hub, while also having spaces for community groups and clubs (boxing, ballet etc), was seen more as a place to interface with local services. The Trinity Centre, however, is perceived as 'owned' by the community.

> *We have a physical advantage, we are a very iconic building. As a church we've tried to make sure we keep our buildings high quality and we get very little vandalism. It is a very well-used*

building which children and families use – we hope that they know where their bread's buttered!

Church member/leader (North Ormesby)

Both centres were being used extensively, and the leaderships of the Hub and the Centre collaborate where they can (as with the youth project mentioned in chapter 2). Their ongoing existence should be seen as one reason why North Ormesby, although very deprived, retains a sense of community and stability.

One church community centre, even one run as effectively and imaginatively as the Trinity Centre, can't do everything, nor should it try to. Some things are appropriately placed elsewhere.

Some interviewees voiced fears that further cuts in Middlesbrough Council's budget could affect the Hub. If that were the case, then the Trinity Centre wouldn't and couldn't do everything done at the Hub (e.g., library services, internet access, work clubs). In other words, it was important that the two facilities were working in tandem. With the badge 'community building', they are perceived as doing similar things. One church community centre, even one run as effectively and imaginatively as the Trinity Centre, can't do everything, nor should it try to. Some things are appropriately placed elsewhere.

The other case studies faced a different set of challenges altogether.

In Byker, the future use and development of their building loomed large in the thoughts of the church leaders. On the one hand, it was iconic in the area – its presence was one of the reasons why no significant community spaces were designed at the time when Byker was being redeveloped in the 1960s and 1970s.[6] There was a strong desire to use it for the wider benefit of the community – for their growing youth projects, for example – and to improve it for the church. On the other hand, the state of the building, and the size of the task in making it fit and flexible for community use was daunting.

> *One of my big frustrations is the church building that we're in now and the journey to develop that building. This piece of work needs a lot of my attention and energy and that's in tension with more pressing things elsewhere. We're excited about using it more and opening it up, but in terms of trying to develop the rest of the building it feels like an uphill struggle... It's about having a vision and going for it, but you feel like the stacks are against us in terms of the kind money we'll need. A community like ours is never going to be able to raise that kind of money.*

Church leader, Case Study B

There is an added complication with the geography of Byker. The neighbourhood descends toward the Tyne in a steep enough incline for people to be unwilling to travel 'up the bank'. This felt like an internal geographical barrier – one which was also affecting the work of the adjacent community centre.

Meanwhile the church's shop front space – the Cross Café – while located at the centre of Byker, suffered from being small and limited in terms of facilities. Indeed, while the original vision for its development had been for a general café used widely by the community, it now functions mainly as a drop-in space for different groups (particularly an after school crowd). Even here, however, space limitations mean it would struggle to host more many more than a dozen children at a time.

After hours, the Cross Café becomes the space for the church's youth activities – Youth Café and Youth Café Extra – on midweek evenings, though again these can accommodate only a limited number. The impression overall is of a space being worked very hard and that many of the activities would benefit from more and better facilities and differentiated spaces. The Cross Café would struggle to be a place, for instance, of genuine social mixing, given there might only be room for a couple of families in there at one time.

Shildon faces similar challenges. Community spaces (at least those in the town centre) are small, and facilities are limited. The church's project Shildon Alive is fortunate to have a building of its own. The church, while in a good state of repair, would not be a suitable home for what they do.

> *If we didn't have a building we'd really struggle. A lot of the time the church is taken up with other activities that you couldn't cross over with something else going on. The upstairs space is brilliant but you couldn't have people milling around outside when there's a funeral happening. St John's is beautiful but it isn't really practical.*

Project manager, Case Study A

The project's location on the high street was also seen as an advantage. Interviewees told us that most people knew where it was and how to access it. Again, however, it is a small space and can't comfortably accommodate more than a few people at a time. As mentioned in chapter 2, one of the strengths in the neighbourhood – and particularly of Shildon Alive – is a large bank of engaged volunteers. The project manager had been obliged to start a rota for staff in order to make it clear when they would – and more importantly, when they would not – be in the Hub.

> *We want a bigger premises, I could do with my own office. People have no sense of privacy, they'll come in the office and sometimes I'll have people in there crying.*

Project worker, Case Study A

However, the project has been able to have a footprint much larger than its premises. Public spaces are not only spaces inside four walls. Their gardening clubs and guerrilla gardening initiatives engaged a large number of children from the local schools, as well as older residents.

Room for improvement

Public spaces that draw people to engage with each other and with issues of common concern, are important for neighbourhood resilience. In an online age, physical spaces are still vital in encouraging people to act together and support each other.

In each of our three case studies, these spaces were at a premium. Where they were present, they were also often limited in size and facilities, which kept community activities small, and made it difficult to offer basic levels of support. During our visit, Shildon Alive were looking to move into bigger premises – the former doctor's surgery opposite the church. However,

Public spaces that draw people to engage with each other and with issues of common concern, are important for neighbourhood resilience. In an online age, physical spaces are still vital in encouraging people to act together and support each other.

NHS property services said they were not able to lease the property, and could not "sell 'off market' to non-public sector organisations". Shildon Alive tried to raise sufficient funds to bid for the property at the public auction, but were unsuccessful.[7]

Churches are stewards of certain public spaces. These range from large multipurpose community centres, to small shop front spaces, to the churches themselves. However, thought and creativity is required to develop what are often large Victorian (or older) buildings, in varying states of repair, into spaces that can be used for worship in all its forms. Not many Church of England vicars sign up out of a passion for the management and development of heritage properties. The question, therefore, is what support can be made available through any institutions that recognise the importance of public space – whether these are diocesan church structures, organisations such as the National Churches Trust[8], or 'secular' public authorities.

When it comes to resilience, neighbourhoods can't be expected to make bricks without straw.

Appropriately sized, located and funded public spaces build resilience, but public space is being 'privatised'. More needs to be done to reserve, create and sustain these spaces – when it comes to resilience, neighbourhoods can't be expected to make bricks without straw.

1 Amy Plender, *After Grenfell: the Faith Groups' Response* (Theos, 2018), p. 46.

2 Dan Gregory, *Skittled out? The collapse and revival of England's social infrastructure* (Local Trust, 2018).

3 www.trinitycentre.org/The%20Trinity%20Centre%20Vision.pdf

4 www.themagichatcafe.co.uk/

5 Eric O Jacobson, *The Space Between: A Christian Engagement with the Built Environment* (Baker Academic, 2012).

6 The architect Ralph Erskine did include 84 'hobby rooms' – small spaces that could be used for crafts or workshops. Some of these are now being converted into residential dwellings, while most remain out of use. No-one mentioned these during our visits to Byker.

7 Kris Jepson, 'Shildon Alive community hub searching for bigger home', *ITV News*, 2 February 2018. www.itv.com/news/tyne-tees/2018-02-02/shildon-alive-community-hub-searching-for-bigger-home/

8 www.nationalchurchestrust.org/

4
Purpose

CHAPTER 4 SUMMARY

— Relatively deprived communities are often dominated by narratives of decline. These stories may be true but they are also limited, trapping areas in their own past and preventing adaption and learning. They are resistance stories rather than resilience stories, 'if only' stories, rather than 'what if' stories.

— Low spiritual capital can result in insularity, low aspiration, and disengagement.

— Churches self-consciously tackled decline stories with future stories, public celebration, internal diversity and a focus on change over time.

GK Chesterton once said, "Men did not love Rome because she was great. She was great because they had loved her."[1] Perhaps this works in reverse too. Can neighbourhoods slide because people think, feel or say they're finished, and that everything that was worthwhile about the place is in the past?

In the past, local authorities in the North East adopted the policy of refusing to support communities they felt were economically unsustainable. None of the neighbourhoods we looked at fell into any such category, though local labour markets radically changed in the 1960s, '70s, '80s and '90s. The Swan Hunter shipyard in Wallsend (neighbouring Byker) closed in 1994 and Shildon rail works in

> **Can neighbourhoods slide because people think, feel or say they're finished, and that everything that was worthwhile about the place is in the past?**

1984. But Byker is within walking distance of Newcastle City Centre, or minutes on the Metro. Shildon is a short train ride away from Darlington.

Although our three case study neighbourhoods have entrenched social problems, they should not be seen as hopeless places – but there is a sense that people do see them this way.

> *Low aspirations here are linked to when the works closed. It ripped the heart out of the community. It wasn't just a job, they provided people with a social life... and people would holiday together. When that institution went it devastated the community, people look back to it as a golden time. The town was more prosperous financially and socially. We need to look to the future but lots of people look backwards.*
>
> **Church leader, Case Study A**

> *There's no reason to come here workwise. It's not like anybody's coming for anything other than a large house that they can rent reasonably priced.*
>
> **Headteacher, Case Study A**

> *When we first moved here my daughter said "Dad look at the people". When you walk along the street it's easy to be struck by the number of people who appear defeated. Overweight, shabby clothes. People look older than they are.*
>
> **Church leader, Case Study A**

> *Everything seems to be bleak. Not only for people in the community but the church as well.*
>
> **Church volunteer, Case Study B**

It's not really been very good over the years. Some youth can be quite cheeky and rough. Basically noisy. It's noisy where I live at the minute, used to have problems with noisy neighbours, settled down at the minute. It's gone downhill a lot over the years.

Interviewer: What was it like before?

Oh it was lovely. But the past five or six years it's not the same as what it used to be

Project volunteer, Case Study B

There is a risk, of course, in identifying genuine problems as 'narratives', as if someone shouldn't be fussing about getting their windows smashed in or being sanctioned at the benefits office. However, there is a process of 'meaning-making', which has been shown to be significant for individual resilience. This process can be interpersonal and collective.

If only vs. what if

There are different stories about the meaning of what is happening to a neighbourhood. What kind of story is winning out? "This could be a decent community, *if only...* we hadn't lost those jobs, we got the investment and attention that they do elsewhere", and so on. These 'stories' cast what is happening within the neighbourhood as almost irrelevant. Change can only come from outside. The dissenting story points in a different direction. "This could be a decent place to live. *What if...* we could train people in better money

> There is a process of 'meaning-making', which has been shown to be significant for individual resilience. This process can be interpersonal and collective.

management, help start a community land trust, run the best youth work around...?"

Communities and institutions where the latter story is winning have a much higher quotient of spiritual capital. They offer, in one word, hope – but hoping against what? It's worth thinking about the effects of this collective meaning-making if the *if only* stories win out.

First, this can result in a sense of local identity which appears strong, but is also brittle. An area might have strong 'bonding' capital – where there is solidarity amongst similar people – but weak 'bridging' capital – where people welcome, relate to and work with people different from them. Bonding capital is associated with *resistance* to change – but resistance is not the same as resilience. A BME interviewee spoke of his experience of outright hostility.

> First when I came, I thought this is not a place for someone to live who is a foreigner. There are people who were ignorant, add to that other people are nasty, racist... They throw stones, call you names, throw eggs. And the people on the bus will sit away from you. You feel lonely and isolated.

Community partner, Case Study B

In this case study, many interviewees spoke of the disadvantages of being perceived as an outsider. Another interview spoke of his context as "racist and homophobic". In the light of everything the area felt it had lost, it had turned inward: "People lose the sense that they're part of something bigger... I think simply because one way of protecting the centre is to identify those who are other and to use them to say 'well, we're not like them' and reinforce an identity."

This is one element of the high Brexit vote in the North East.[2] Church communities in our case study neighbourhoods were genuinely the most diverse institutions in the area. They were a point of connection and welcome for immigrants and asylum seekers (even those of other religions), and were also relatively diverse in terms of social class.

Second, the word 'aspiration' – or, more to the point, low aspirations – was important in all three case studies. The word has associations with the politics of social mobility – with getting on and getting out – but here it was used to describe a broader feeling of lives without purpose. A local councillor in the same case study spoke of a "knock on effect with kids, if they see this negativity in life, they aren't going to aspire to do anything". All three case study churches spoke to this theme in their work with families with young children.

Third, if aspiration was a belief in a future with purpose, there was also a sense that people couldn't make a difference in the present – a feeling of disengagement. In chapter 2 we discussed the challenge of encouraging and training local leaders, whether for church-based roles or public facing community projects. A personal lack of confidence was a barrier to overcome. There was a lack of confidence in neighbourhoods as a whole – affecting not just the vulnerable, the marginalised and the young but also the leaders who were genuinely committed to 'making a difference'.

If aspiration was a belief in a future with purpose, there was also a sense that people couldn't make a difference in the present.

> *We've got third, fourth generation unemployed now. That's a*
> *tough nut to crack. I think there's a lot of people trying to do good*
> *work but the problem's almost too big.*
>
> **Headteacher, Case Study A**

One church leader (Case Study A) described being struck on arrival in his post by "the number of people who appear defeated... There's a reluctance to take responsibility because they don't believe they can". People looked back to higher levels of employment in the area, but the effect of those single employer economies was also negative – people, in his word, were "institutionalised". Later he reflected, "I feel almost as if my role has been saying to people 'yes you can', giving people permission almost."

Building spiritual capital

In a 2012 report on the role of English Cathedrals we argued that

> *[By] recognising and guiding emergent spiritualities; by*
> *bringing together different groups from across an area; by*
> *receiving and welcoming the whole community on special*
> *occasions; by choreographing and adding dignity and solemnity*
> *to moments of grief or celebration; by embodying the very*
> *identity and tradition of a city and locality... cathedrals offer a*
> *unique resource for contemporary England.*[3]

This is not unique to cathedrals. Local church communities can do the same thing for their neighbourhood. In other words, they can build local spiritual capital. This spiritual capital is a stockpile of hope, activism and purpose.

Churches and other religious organisations are well-placed to understand the importance of spiritual capital, and consciously to build up a neighbourhood's reserves. The substance of Christian convictions is deeply important, though not in the sense that churches are looking for individual conversions. There was a, 'yes, but...' feel to what many of the interviewees said about the religious nature of church action: *yes*, people's faith is important in what they do *but* it's not experienced in an exclusive or hostile way.

> *The faith aspect comes in, Jesus was here to help everybody whether they believe it or not. No need to quote scriptures and Bibles...We work exceptionally closely with the church but it's not the be all and end all of the project. It's the underlying 'we will help everybody'... We are part of the church but one step away, it creates that diversity to keep it not too religious and help everybody.*
>
> **Project worker, Case Study A**

Are churches achieving this inclusive culture by toning down their religiosity or hiding the theological commitments that serve as a source of motivation for their work? No – these commitments were still very much present, but leaders were bridging from core Christian commitments into the social and political realities. They were working out the implications of their tradition in a complex context, aware of the ways in which communities were materially and psychologically vulnerable.

> *What is the gospel? I think you have to begin with original blessing – the love of God first. Sin is so much in people's face. They already feel such a failure in life. It's not where we begin.*
>
> **Church leader, Case Study C**

Although it isn't the primary factor of building spiritual capital, it is a factor. One project volunteer, who had in the past been a beneficiary, spoke about the importance of faith in her own life. Christianity and the church helped her tap reserves of spiritual capital in very adverse circumstances.

> *I found faith because of PTSD. I suffered trauma and through that I found my faith all over again and grabbed on to the hope of that because someone that I loved passed away. They had to go to heaven, that's the only way I could answer it. I was determined that God was sending signs, reaching out saying He was listening... I've got no family round me, but the church is my family. I do feel like I belong in that church, I'm welcome in that church and anyone I know is. There is faith here, and hope here.*

There were plenty of others who were engaged in volunteering but had not joined the church. It would still not be right, however, to describe them as having a 'secular' outlook. Again, church, religion and faith occupied a paradoxical place – they were acknowledged as problematic or just irrelevant for many, but also as essential for the holistic nature of church-based responses.

> *We're offering more than food, than physical mentoring – emotional and spiritual health as well. But not in your face. In a way that's more attainable, achievable for people who may not be ready yet to be in a church building...We're not trying to be nothing we're not, not trying to be clever, just trying to be real.*
> ### Church and project volunteer, Case Study B

This raises the question, is 'spiritual capital' a preserve of those who ascribe to formal religious traditions? No... and yes. One community centre worker started her interview by announcing her atheism, "Except people... I refuse to give up with people". She was as invested in the well-being of the community as anyone else, but she was eager to point out differentiate her motivation. This motivation was meaningful to her, but explicitly rejected the shared narratives or meanings that would characterise faith-based social engagement. If it is anything, then spiritual capital must be a *shared* sense of meaning and purpose.

Beyond the question of religious ethos, we felt that building spiritual capital rested on the way that churches narrated the past and spoke about the future.

Memory and celebration

Churches everywhere hold community fun days or church fetes. These are probably seen as sitting on the very 'fluffy' end of faith-based social action, with debt advice, benefits advocacy and the rest at the other. This view underplays the importance of a local sense of identity and purpose, which in turn underpins the belief that there is an 'us'.

In 2008, the Trinity Centre celebrated the history of their own church, but not of the church building. Their 'Living Stones' festival celebrated the community of faith who over 150 years have found meaning, purpose and peace through the church. The festivities lasted a whole year, and brought 28 groups and organisations and hundreds of local people of all ages together to learn about their heritage and celebrate their community. From an instrumental context, the project was vital in building relationships which would develop further with initiatives like the Big Local. The significance, however, was wider than that – the estimated ward rank for North Ormesby in the 2015 Index of Multiple Deprivation is 2, with 1 being the most deprived (down from 7 in 2010). A festival like this helps to contradict the despair around such statistics.

A more recent example could be seen in Shildon. Last year, local children were invited to contribute 100 words about someone who 'lit up' their lives. The submissions had to be about ordinary people, rather than a celebrity of sportsperson. These were then published in a book – 173 young people made contributions with stories about friends and family members. After the book (*Burning Bright: An Anthology of Love, Lived in Shildon*) was published, the church organised lantern building workshops. Later, they carried the lanterns through the town and released them in a local park, symbolising the presence of 'light' in Shildon.

> *If people hear noise on a night it's usually 'what on earth's going on', but it was happy, everyone was having a good time. We had a really positive reaction.*

Project worker, Case Study A

This points to the significance of local culture as a means to influence the geographical psychology. It is therefore a space in which churches can and should be active. The Kynren festival which runs at Auckland Castle – a stone's throw from Shildon – should be seen in this light. The event – a tour through 2000 years of English/County Durham history (though including mythical elements) has attracted bemusement from some national commentators (the "bonkers" product of the "madcap mind" of City fund manager Jonathan Ruffer, in the words of one report).[4] 'Bonkers' though these things may be, to not have them is to yield the symbolic world to forms of populism which don't tell a story of hope but of resentment and therefore necessary disruption.

Narrating the future

Finally, in all three case studies it struck us that youth work, partnerships with schools, and a focus on local families were important. The Trinity Centre Youth and Children's work was regarded by one community partner as "probably the best in Middlesbrough, maybe even the rest of Teesside". With limited resources, St Michael's Byker was engaging young people, whether in their café/shop front space or with 'detached teams', and seeing young people in church on a Sunday morning. In one way or another, a large proportion of children were in contact with Shildon Alive – the Burning Bright project, community and guerrilla gardens, and engagement in financial education. Interviewees here reported cynicism about the trees they had planted – "they'll get pulled down in no time" – but engaging young people in the development of the orchards and gardens meant that they would connect with their town in a different way.

In all three case studies it struck us that youth work, partnerships with schools, and a focus on local families were important.

Churches are often thought of as orientated towards the past. That is not quite correct, or at least it wasn't when it came to our case study neighbourhoods. Churches naturally occupy time as well as space. Local people – even those who aren't closely associated with the church, might have been married there or baptised in the church. There is a natural association across generations – including present and future generations.

It also makes pragmatic sense for them to work with young people when dealing with some of the ingrained social problems present in these neighbourhoods. One interviewee, speaking about the struggles people were having with "fuel, food and finance" drew attention to financial literacy work they were doing in schools. "Really, we'll know if we've been successful in twenty years. We're helping them in the future". The stories of young people's lives should not be determined ahead of time.

> *We're not naïve about the challenges here. We live amongst it all the time. Neither will we buy into this completely negative story about this community because there are lots and lots of positives. When we asked young people what they want, they said we want space to have fun, to learn skills and [to have an] opportunity to give back to the community. They're exemplary answers. Don't tar us all with this brush.*
>
> **Church project worker, Case Study C**

Spiritual regeneration

It is commonplace to think about economic regeneration – and also economic resilience – and we have a sense of what some of the relevant tools and approaches might be (improving housing, encouraging businesses, creating transport links, and so on).

The language of spiritual capital draws attention to the importance of non-tangible factors of identity, culture and expectation. It is important to say that spiritual capital is not the preserve of religious people or institutions. However, they are well-placed to understand and contribute to it.

Theologian David Ford writes of the nature of life as one of ongoing "multiple overwhelming" – this is a necessary and inevitable process of change and challenge but one that can be interpreted as a blessing, even if not a comfortable process.[5] For Ford, death and resurrection are the paradigmatic example of this multiple overwhelming in the Christian faith – and determinative of Christian mission and action. Within such a story pessimism can be defied, and not only by trite optimism which ignores or dismisses suffering. Churches in our neighbourhoods are consciously opposing pessimism, hopelessness, powerlessness, and exclusion, weaving celebration and gratitude into the life of their community. They are helping people hope.

This is not merely an instruction for vulnerable communities to cheer up. Nor is it a replacement for concrete social, physical and economic interventions. Rather, these churches are contributing to the 'spiritual regeneration' of a neighbourhood.

Churches in our neighbourhoods are consciously opposing pessimism, hopelessness, powerlessness, and exclusion, weaving celebration and gratitude into the life of their community. They are helping people hope.

1 GK Chesterton, *Orthodoxy* (New Kensington: Whitaker House, 2013), p. 46.

2 Daniel Wright, 'People pushed to the margins driven to vote for Brexit', *Joseph Rowntree Foundation*, 31 August 2016. www.jrf.org.uk/press/people-pushed-margins-driven-vote-brexit

3 Theos and The Grubb Institute, *Spiritual Capital: the Present and Future of English Cathedrals*, (Theos, 2012), p. 60.

4 Ruth Sutherland, 'Meet the philanthropic fund guru who splashed £30m of his own cash on the most bonkers show in Britain', *This is Money*, 20 June 2016. www.thisismoney.co.uk/money/news/article-3651062/Meet-philanthropic-fund-guru-splashed-30m-cash-bonkers-Britain.html

5 David Ford, *The Shape of Living: Spiritual Directions for Everyday Life* (Grand Rapids MI: Baker Books, 2004).

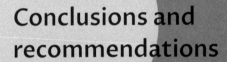

Conclusions and recommendations

Church-based community action is significant in both size and scope – and ever more so. In the North East, many churches operate in contexts of overwhelming social challenge, manifested in material deprivation and a sense of pessimism and purposelessness.

As national institutions churches still have significant social (and economic) power; at the neighbourhood level, however, they face significant constraints. In the next few years, resources are likely to be stretched even further. Deprived communities – particularly those in the North East – are not going to experience a Brexit dividend but a Brexit surcharge. Churches already doing their best to respond to high levels of need may themselves be overwhelmed as some areas – again, particularly the North East – will suffer a potentially severe economic set back and the loss of European Structural and Social Funding.

Any wishful thinking about churches resuming their role as a, still less 'the', core social provider must be treated with caution.

Pragmatically, at the local/neighbourhood level there is no real possibility of increasing the quantity of charitable and voluntary action to an extent where they can simply balance out these challenges, nor 'plug the gap' as local and other public authorities operate under their own constraints. Any wishful thinking about churches resuming their role as a, still less 'the', core social provider must be treated with caution. All the churches worked with for this research are doing good work, but all of them experience constraints, whether in funding or facilities.

Churches are (sometimes) resilient institutions, but it is not for them to reclaim the social realm as if it were a deserted building. Rather they should see themselves as one amongst many community actors. Part of this must be about understanding the pathways to greater neighbourhood resilience, and understanding the distinctive ways in which churches might be able to define them.

In other words, churches should be thinking seriously about how they can contribute to neighbourhood resilience. Although the term has been used in vague or even unhelpful ways, the nexus of people (social capital), places (physical capital) and purpose (spiritual capital) represents a development of the term that is both rigorous and meaningful for churches and faith-based organisations. As we have seen, each 'domain' can be further differentiated, even into firm indicators, which could be used to take a snapshot of the churches' contribution to neighbourhood resilience, or possibly even track resilience over time. How can resilience be embedded into the work of churches?

Recommendation 1: A simple church-based resilience tool could be developed to help churches think about their community's vulnerabilities and potential and assess their own contribution. This could support decision-making around mission action plans.

Recommendation 2: Resilience measures can be used to inform the allocation of resources within denominations. These should complement measures of relative deprivation or absolute poverty.

Recommendation 3: Resilience 'best practice' should be used to inform ministerial education and formation. Specific training could be delivered around the three 'domains' – people, places, purpose. Key skills include community development and volunteer management.

People

Our case study neighbourhoods were not civil society 'cold-spots'. Indeed, if anything they were 'hot spots', often subject to well-meaning but short-term interventions or bureaucratic tinkering. One interviewee spoke about how a youth charity came with an aspiration to develop mental health services in their neighbourhood. "They did all the hard work of building relationships with the families, and then the funding ran out and they left. That's frustrating for the families, and they won't trust people so easily again".

The point of this domain is that resilience is something that 'comes up' from the neighbourhood itself, as people are cared for, as they grow, serve and eventually lead. As genuinely local institutions act with common purpose, so resilience develops. In its essence, it is not about meeting needs but about summoning people to be all that they can be. It is a well-worn claim, but churches are not merely hospitals – they are also schools.

> **Resilience is something that 'comes up' from the neighbourhood itself, as people are cared for, as they grow, serve and eventually lead. As genuinely local institutions act with common purpose, so resilience develops.**

From a Christian perspective, resilience could be understood as a hard-headed form of love of neighbour. To adopt the parable, it removes the victim from the ditch, binds his wounds and gets him to a place of recovery. But it doesn't force him to stay in the bed but looks to his full healing and independence.

The same approach should influence institutional decision-making. Local civic action can be deep, sustained and transformative. It can also be fragmented and superficial. This is not a matter of the size or the turnover of an organisation, but of their intent and quality. The churches are 'sold' on community action – this is not a matter of whether or not. It is a matter of what and how. Deep and intentional collaboration is the only option. What ways could this characterise church-based public action?

> *Recommendation 4: Though there will always be a need for 'first aid' responses, where possible churches should move away from give-away charitable models. The purpose is not conditionality or disciplining the recipient, but recognising dignity, building relationship and encouraging agency. For example, food cooperatives, pay-as-you-feel, and community supermarkets represent positive innovations in the food poverty world.*

> *Recommendation 5: Although churches are clear that they want to embrace 'with and alongside' approaches to community action and avoid 'for and to' approaches, it is difficult to identify and train local leaders, whether for work inside or outside of congregations. National church bodies need to lead by example, and reshape ministerial recruitment and training practices so that they are open to those from diverse socio-economic and educational backgrounds.*

> *Recommendation 6: For the most part churches are collaborative in their work, but they're not yet making the most of every opportunity for collective action with diverse others. Community organising supports collaborative political action, though not necessarily collaborative social action. Churches and others should work together to establish neighbourhood*

partnerships – already in place in some cities nationally –
bringing together community groups, local representatives,
business leaders. These could ease information sharing, or enable
formal partnerships for collective bids to run local services.

Place

Common spaces are important for neighbourhood
resilience, though they need to be effectively used. Yet they
are being lost at a worrying rate. Many community spaces
are small and not fit for purpose. Church buildings can be
important social structures but they are not always suitable for
community use. Often they are nineteenth century buildings,
at best struggling to deliver twentieth century priorities,
never mind twenty-first century needs. It is often left to the
creativity of local leaders to make a plan, build a case and
source funding for a development – almost an impossible task.

Unlike the neighbourhood and community programmes
under New Labour, there is currently no funding for the
development of community spaces. This throws the ball back
into the court of voluntary groups who maintain public spaces,
and whatever private philanthropy is available to support their
development. There is a broader public stake in making sure
communities have the right kinds of facilities to meet needs.

We need to take measures to understand and support the
existing 'social infrastructure' and find resources to fill the
ever-expanding gaps.

Recommendation 7: Local authorities should conduct
neighbourhood audits of community facilities. This could be used
to inform how services are planned and delivered, but could also
identify gaps in provision. Local authorities and others should

build on and support facilities that are already there, including churches.

Recommendation 8: Spaces like schools and health centre spaces should be made available to community agencies where there is sufficient alignment in mission. When new facilities (e.g., schools or health centres) are being constructed, an up-to-date community facility audit could identify opportunities to develop larger community hubs combining various services and community activities. Public sector policies on off-market sales of assets should be reviewed to ensure they are achieving the best outcomes for communities, with the possible extension of Community Asset Transfer approaches, which are already in place for local authorities.

Recommendation 9: Churches should give more attention to developing church-owned spaces as potential spaces for revenue generation. More support and advice should be available for churches seeking to renew or develop existing buildings for community-focused purposes.

Recommendation 10: To make significant new funds available, a new Community Wealth Fund – similar to sovereign wealth funds – could be established. In the US, Reimagining the Civic Commons (civiccommons.us) is investing in five cities – Akron, Chicago, Detroit, Memphis, and Philadelphia – to upgrade existing infrastructure to reflect 21st-century needs. In the UK, a Shale Wealth Fund is already being developed to support communities near shale gas extraction sites. The Community Wealth Fund could be funded through multiple sources – the proposed post-Brexit shared prosperity fund, dormant assets, or an endowment. It could focus on areas vulnerable to the negative outcomes of Britain's departure from the European Union.

Purpose

We started by asking why similarly deprived neighbourhoods experience different outcomes. One of the 'variables' that will affect this is a neighbourhood's culture, morale, identity and meaning-making. This sense of itself is what we have called its spiritual capital.

All neighbourhoods will have commonly exchanged stories or narratives: the question is, are they narratives of decline or narratives of hope? Indeed, just as certain kinds of social outcome can have negative outcomes, so can certain kinds of spiritual capital.

> **All neighbourhoods will have commonly exchanged stories or narratives: the question is, are they narratives of decline or narratives of hope?**

Though the concept might feel a little intangible, its outcomes are not. Seemingly strong but ultimately fragile identities resulting in insularity and hostility to the other, cynicism, low aspirations, disengagement and the sense of frustration that creates fertile ground for nationalism and populism. Churches can help rebuild spiritual capital by acts of celebration and telling a more hopeful story about the future – not one of blithe optimism, but one of the possibility of change over time. Their own ethnic diversity is an important witness, as is the fact that they are committed to intergenerational presence.

Spiritual capital is not merely the reserve of religious organisations or individuals, but they are well-placed to build it on a national and local level.

Recommendation 11: Churches and church-based institutions – including funders – should continue to operate on an extended time frame, and emphasise working with young people on projects which build skills and aspirations.

Recommendation 12: The Church of England in particular is well-positioned to help build an inclusive and positive national identity. Churches need to engage with conversations around culture, identity and particularly Englishness as enthusiastically as they do on issues of poverty and exclusion.

Conclusion

We have argued that a resilience perspective would represent an important development in thinking around church-based social action. In a context where churches and faith-based organisations are themselves facing considerable disruption, yet are increasingly being re-woven into the fabric of social provision, churches need alternative ways to understand and steer their own work.

A commitment to resilience should see churches or charities focus on building people up rather than on meeting material needs. The North East faces serious challenges. If they develop as anticipated, these challenges may overwhelm churches that themselves are often small, marginal, and poorly resourced. Churches will need to keep themes of responsibility, agency, common action and leadership in sight. These causes are deeper and more difficult than simple material provision – and churches are right to search for different ways forward. Structuring action around attempts to build social, physical and spiritual capital may be one way forward.

A commitment to resilience should see churches or charities focus on building people up rather than on meeting material needs.

A final word on the limits of resilience. One of its most popular definitions is the ability to beat the odds. A large number of our interviewees – both church and secular – wanted to emphasise the need not to 'beat the odds' but to 'change the odds'. If resilience does rely on a vision of hope, this is exactly the kind of message the residents of Byker, North Ormesby and Shildon need to hear.

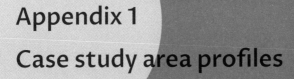

Appendix 1
Case study area profiles

Byker

Byker is an electoral ward situated in East Newcastle, close to the city centre. The Byker Estate within this is famous as the setting of the children's TV programme, Byker Grove. It was once a warren of Victorian working-class terraced houses with a close-knit population of around 17,000.

In the 1960s it was earmarked for destruction as part of the slum clearances taking place throughout Britain. The estate was redesigned by Ralph Erskine who introduced innovative architectural ideas such as the Byker Wall. This is a block of apartments which looms above surrounding buildings and marks the edge of the estate. Originally intended to buffer the community from a planned motorway that never came to fruition, it is now a Grade II listed building. The estate's renovation was intended to involve residents and reduce disruption to their lives as much as possible, however, many were moved out of the area during demolition and few returned when rebuilding was complete – some statistics put the return rate at as little as 20% of original residents with the population in 2015 estimated at around 9,500.[1] The close-knit community relationships that had built up as generations lived and died together were irreparably damaged by this dislocation and the once strong community identity was undermined.

The Byker area now experiences high population turnover with residents often concerned about security and safety in the area – only 53% said they feel safe in the area after dark – as well as few opportunities for employment. Compared to the national average, Byker has a higher percentage of residents with no qualifications, residents claiming benefits, and residents in lower social grades.[2]

Crime is an increasingly significant issue, especially anti-social behaviour among youth which is possibly aggravated by the distinct lack of places for young people to go or things for them to do.[3] Statistics released by Newcastle Council put the number of under 16s living in poverty at 54.1% – far above the Newcastle average of 29.9% and the national average of 21.2%. Byker ranks second on the Index of Multiple Deprivation out of a collection of 26 wards.[4]

The community largely lives in social housing which is owned and maintained by Byker Community Trust. The Trust has an office in the Byker Estate, next to a small collection of community aid organisations offering cheap food, company, and volunteering opportunities. One of these, African Community Advice North East, reflects the multi-cultural nature of Byker – 10% of residents here identify as 'non-white'.[5] Other community assets include the estate's two primary schools – rated Ofsted Outstanding and Good respectively – and good, relatively cheap, transport links to the city centre.

Shildon

Shildon is a small town situated two miles south-east of Bishop Auckland in County Durham. It owes its existence to the presence of nearby coal mines which offered multiple generations relatively stable work during the 18th and 19th centuries. The Stockton and Darlington Railway was opened in 1825 in order to quickly transport coal from Shildon collieries to the port in Stockton. This railway put Shildon on the map; it was the world's first public steam railway and the engineers working on it paved the way for modern railways. One notable example is Timothy Hackworth, after whom many of the town's assets are named.

Shildon residents relied heavily on these two industries – coal and rail – for employment. On the one hand, this engendered a close sense of community. Throughout adulthood, everybody worked long shifts together, walked to and from work together and lived close to each other. According to some sources, this bred insularity and suspicion towards outsiders which further strengthened community bonds. On the other hand, economic reliance on these industries caused vulnerability. When the coal mines and wagon works were closed at the end of the 20th century, masses of residents were launched into unemployment. The town faced economic downturn, and many moved away in search of jobs thereby damaging the town's social fabric too.

Shildon currently has a population of around 10,000 people. Most are UK-born and, compared to the national average, older, less qualified, more likely to be unemployed and more likely to claim benefits. Those who do have jobs tend to work in 'elementary occupations' for example as bar staff or machine operators.[6] There are a number of churches in Shildon – CofE, Catholic, Methodist and Salvation Army – but like churches nationally, attendance is limited and as the vast majority of residents identify as either 'Christian' or 'non-religious'. Visibility of other religious groups is minimal.

Reminders of Shildon's accomplished past are visible throughout the town centre – rail wagons bedecked with flowers, impressive iron archways reminiscent of railway tracks marking each end of the high street, and a critically acclaimed railway museum – but little has been done to develop a new identity in the town. Few businesses are invested – no supermarkets, post offices or even banks – and the only well-known franchise on the high street is a relatively spacious Costa Coffee. Community organisations such as Shildon Alive are often the only places for residents to access services such as internet job searches, benefits advice, skills training and free food parcels. Ironically, given the town's railway past, transport links with surrounding towns and cities are poor.

However, it isn't all doom and gloom. Shildon possesses some valuable assets including three primary schools – two rated Ofsted Outstanding, one Good – and one secondary school, a large park with space for children to play, and a leisure centre located relatively centrally.

North Ormesby

North Ormesby – also known as 'Doggy' – is an electoral
ward in Middlesbrough situated to the east of the town centre.
Its population boomed in the mid-19th century, mainly due to
large iron mines and the resultant ironworks factories located
nearby – those employed here came to live in the area. Its
nickname is thought to derive from the 'wet dog' smell emitted
from the ironworks, though many other explanations have also
been given.[7]

In recent decades the area has experienced decline –
service cuts and reductions – and population figures have
decreased to around 3,000 people.[8] This is partly due to the
closure of the mines in the late 20th century, causing many
residents to move out of the area in search of work. Another
major contributor was the building of Riverside Stadium, home
to Middlesbrough FC, and the busy A66 road, which caused
large areas of housing to be demolished. Although the stadium
attracts thousands of people, few actually enter North Ormesby
and therefore businesses benefit little. Furthermore, although
the A66 improves links with other areas, it also isolates North
Ormesby from Middlesbrough centre as the heavy traffic makes
it difficult to cross.

One third of North Ormesby's residents have lived there
for more than 20 years. However, another third have been
there for less than three.[9] What was once a tight-knit and
desirable community now consists – at least in part – of "low
cost, poor quality housing [for] people, many of whom have
no former connection here".[10] Compared to national averages,
high proportions of North Ormesby residents are claiming
some form of benefits, are situated in lower social grades,
and are leaving school without any qualifications. Crime –
largely anti-social behaviour – levels are high leading to many

residents feeling unsafe in the area, especially at night. In some parts, as many as 75% of residents feel that North Ormesby as an area is getting worse and 42% want to move away.[11] A large part of this discontent surrounds unaccountable private landlords who house unruly and disruptive tenants and/or fail to provide acceptable standards of living.[12] Although North Ormesby possesses the cheapest houses in the country (two-bedroom houses start from £30,000[13]) a large proportion of residents live in privately rented accommodation.

The area also possesses some assets. The two primary schools are rated Ofsted Good and Outstanding, and the activities and services on offer at both the Council-funded Community Hub and the Trinity Centre run by Holy Trinity Church are varied, providing for a wide range of ages and needs. The market square – once geographically the central point of the town – has been a core part of the community ever since its inception in the 19th century, and continues to be so today, though footfall appears to have dropped in recent years.[14] Residents report feeling that the area has a sense of community, is homely, and offers "everything you need" in its high street shops which include big brands such as Greggs and Boots.[15]

1　Anna Minton, 'Byker Wall: Newcastle's noble failure of an estate - a history of cities in 50 buildings, day 41' *The Guardian*, 21 May 2015, www.theguardian.com/cities/2015/may/21/byker-wall-newcastles-noble-failure-of-an-estate-a-history-of-cities-in-50-buildings-day-41

2　www.ilivehere.co.uk/statistics-byker-newcastle-upon-tyne-6482.html

3　www.police.uk/northumbria/E8/crime/stats/

4　www.wellbeingforlife.org.uk/sites/default/files/Know%20Your%20Community%20-%20Byker%20ward.pdf

5　Ibid.

6　Livin, *livin Shildon: local offer 2012-2015*, 2016 www.livin.co.uk/media/1135/shildon-summary-plan-word-final-version.pdf

7　Mieka Smiles, 'So why IS Nunthorpe naughty and North Ormesby known as Doggy?' *Teeside Live*, 6 December 2016, www.gazettelive.co.uk/news/teesside-news/nunthorpe-naughty-north-ormesby-known-12276182

8　Middlesbrough Council, *Basic Facts about Middlesbrough*, www.middlesbrough.gov.uk/sites/default/files/Middlesbrough_2015_Election_Ward.pdf

9　*North Ormesby Big Local Community profile and vision* (2014) p. 20. localtrust.org.uk/assets/downloads/profiles/A%20VISION%20FOR%20NORTH%20ORMESBY%20final.pdf

10　Ibid.

11　Ibid., pp. 23-24.

12　Ibid., p. 24.

13　Press Association, 'Middlesbrough town named cheapest place to buy a house – so why do people want to leave?' *The Independent*, 22 March 2015, www.independent.co.uk/news/uk/middlesbrough-town-named-cheapest-place-to-buy-a-house-so-why-do-people-want-to-leave-10125682.html

14　www.northormesbymarket.co.uk/about-us.html

15　*North Ormesby Big Local* (2014) p. 27.

Appendix 2

Theoretical survey
of resilience

Background

The term resilience has become something of a buzzword among policy-makers and academics in recent years. However, it is by no means new. Resilient individuals have been revered in fairy tales and myths for centuries, becoming the focus of academic study in the 1950s. Scientists exploring the causes of mental illness realised that being exposed to "risk factors" did not necessitate an individual developing mental ill-health.[1] In fact, some people were found to be "thriving in the face of formidable odds".[2] Interest turned to investigating causes of such resilience with an eye to applying techniques beyond themselves.[3]

Nowadays, the term, 'resilience' is used in a variety of sometimes apparently contradictory ways.

Etymologically, it stems from the Latin 'resilire' meaning to rebound or bounce back,[4] and is understood as such in the field of economics where systems that "bounce back" to a "fixed and narrowly defined equilibrium" following adversity-causing events called "shocks" or "stressors" are described as resilient.[5] Biologically-speaking however, organisms are resilient to the extent that they change or adapt in order to "thrive under adverse environmental conditions".[6] The field of engineering employs the term differently again – here resilience is "efficiency, constancy and predictability…[or in other words] resistance",[7] that is, it refers to a distinct lack of change.

In this appendix section, various applications of the term 'resilience' in the social world will be mapped.

Resilience in international development

Resilience is promoted as an important part of international development work, especially in relation to disaster preparation and response. According to the UK's Humanitarian Emergency Response Review, the relationship between the two is cyclical in nature; "development is the answer to coping with disaster but getting to development can rely on being able to bounce back from disasters."[8] Ultimately then, resilience in terms of an ability to cope with disasters underpins a country's ability to grow and develop. Consequently, the UK endeavours to place the "creation of resilience at the heart of its approach to long-term development and emergency response" in developing countries.[9]

Short-term aid such as giving food and clothing can be necessary in the immediacy of a crisis. However, it can also engender reliance, remove dignity and be costly for the countries offering aid. Long-term solutions are therefore preferred where possible. Ideally, this would be in the form of tackling the causes of adversity, but this is often easier said than done. Natural disasters resulting from climate change and long-term poverty enabled by corrupt governance require immense power and resources to tackle. Rather than just trying to change circumstances beyond their control, NGOs involved with international development often also try to help communities cope with their lot; that is, they focus on beating the odds not changing them.[10]

The Christian charity Tearfund offers some examples of this in practice. Their work in Ethiopia includes assisting poor communities in the creation of self help groups where members can deposit weekly savings for use in times of difficulty. Operated for the community by the community, these groups offer a life-line in the face of unexpected shocks whilst providing empowerment and limiting reliance on foreign aid.[11] This develops resilience in the community, and it can be seen to contribute to the work of international development, if we understand this to consist at least partly of improving quality of life.

Civil resilience

Resilience is also invoked in relation to developed countries' disaster response and, significantly, prevention. The less a community is negatively impacted by a disaster, the better, and a key part of limiting impact is building civil resilience.

The term 'natural disaster' implies that we humans are innocent victims of unforgiving forces of nature. However, this is untrue. Our actions directly impact the extent of the damage caused by extreme weather. For example, deforestation can increase the negative effects of flooding by removing a significant barrier and mechanism for absorbing water.[12] Hurricane Katrina would have been less catastrophic for those living in New Orleans had the wetlands that provided natural protection not been eliminated in economically-minded improvements to their port.[13]

The extent to which communities and individuals prepare specifically for these events also greatly impacts how they are affected by it. For example, communications service giant BT have a civil resilience team on-hand to enact "effective response plans for major civil emergencies".[14] That is, preparations have been made to ensure that good communication systems are in place in the midst of crises, such as extreme weather, greatly improving emergency services' capacity to respond effectively.

Resilience as the ability to bounce back or resist the negative impact of such shocks is often invoked in this context, however, so is resilience as the capacity to adapt. Often, preparations for future potential disasters build on lessons learnt from past ones. For example, after the events of 9/11 the UK government devised a "national resilience plan" increasing their capacity to deal with comparable tragedies.[15] Similarly, responses to the Cumbrian floods of 2009 were effective because communities had come together to overcome a crisis surrounding Foot and Mouth outbreaks a few years earlier in 2001.[16] Resilience has been described as "a muscle...that must be developed in advance and consistently exercised to be both strong enough to withstand severe challenges and flexible enough to handle a wide range of unpredictable forces".[17]

Regional resilience

Resilience language is also applied to shocks other than natural disasters or tragedies – e.g. economic or social stresses. On a regional level, notions of economic resilience are commonly discussed.

Economies in various regions face similar circumstances – such as a recession – but recover or 'bounce back' with varying degrees of success. For example, research reveals that "overall the southern and eastern regions of [the UK] have tended to be more resilient, apparently able to bounce back strongly even if badly hit by a recession".[18] In contrast, northern and western regions are more affected by such shocks.

Community resilience

Community resilience applies similar questions to community settings – how do some communities fare better than others in the face of adversity? In recent years this has become a particularly relevant question, given the introduction of drastic budget cuts – Sheffield County Council's budget, for example, was reduced by 31% in five years[19] – resulting in the loss or reduction of vital services.[20] For some communities this has brought great adversity, however others have been better able to respond, creating their own initiatives and coming together to fill the gaps caused by service cuts.

Researchers have concocted a list of factors thought to contribute to communities' capacity for resilience. These include the presence of "active citizens" within the community who possess the skills to lead such initiatives and encourage other community members to participate,[21] the presence of individuals who are able to volunteer their time and resources,[22] a diversified economic base that is not overly reliant on a single industry,[23] a physical environment that engenders pride in the community and a shared sense of belonging,[24] and good relations between community members and the local authorities. In fact, relationships are often highlighted as central in the formation of community resilience – people working together, helping each other, and co-ordinating with other organisations in the area and the local authorities to ensure that the needs of the community are met efficiently.[25]

Resilience as a policy tool

In recent years, much attention has focused on helping communities become more resilient and able to better cope with today's harsh economic climate – to the extent that government policies are making use of resilience language.

Employing the notion of community resilience, authorities can encourage communities to take responsibility for their own welfare rather than relying on the state.[26] Some regard this with negativity – it encourages "citizen responsibility to survive within existing social structures" over accepting "state responsibility for addressing the harms causes by the various inequalities resulting from contemporary social organisation".[27] Others see it as simply a solution to a shortage of funds:

> Local Authorities are the main target of austerity...local governments have adaptive ability, they can weather the storm through innovation and creativity to reduce the cost of services without major changes to service levels...[but] this capacity for efficiency savings appears to be exhausted [and] cities are forced to make cuts.[28]

In this context, resilience is a way for local governments to deal with the economic difficulties placed on them by national government and higher authorities. Rather than shirking their responsibilities, local governments could be fulfilling them by encouraging practices and mind-sets that could buffer the impact of unavoidable cuts on the real lives of individuals in the community.

The role of churches in resilience

As evidenced in this report, churches can play a significant role in the promotion of community resilience. For one thing, the religious views they promote can engender positivity and hope, offering individuals interpretive frameworks within which to understand their current struggles as meaningful. In doing so, religions can "equip individuals to withstand shock"[29] – though it is important to note that religious views can also sometimes hinder resilience by "promoting fatalism and blame".[30]

Research suggests that churches can be influential in aiding the development of relationships within and between communities – given that relationships are considered "critical" for the development of community resilience,[31] this is significant. Sharing beliefs with others and participating in religious rituals and ceremonies can engender a shared identity and sense of belonging.[32] One outcome of this can be to 'bridge the gap' between individuals from differing backgrounds, social status and levels of privilege, offering opportunities for the disadvantaged to gain access to resources that would be hard for them to reach ordinarily.[33]

Churches also serve a practical function for the development of community resilience in that their buildings are often positioned visibly and centrally within communities. They are therefore ideally situated to host community events, to be transformed into community hubs and cafes, and to offer shelter or protection in the event of a disaster.[34] Moreover, precisely because of their being located *within* the community, local churches – and other faith groups – are "better attuned to the needs, culture, practices and language of community than large international organisations and benefit from high levels of trust from other local social actors".[35]

Critiques of resilience

The concept of resilience has been applied to a range of circumstances and can provide a significant buffer protecting vulnerable individuals and groups from the impact of adversity. However, a few notes of caution must be made.

We cannot reduce resilience to a list of factors that can be blanket applied or easily uploaded to all communities and situations.[36] Christopherson, Michie and Tyler warn that "we should avoid assuming that the same drivers of change are at work everywhere and if we pull the right levers the appropriate drivers will respond and deliver the required outcomes".[37] For one thing, communities differ greatly in

terms of the resources they possess and consequently respond
to shocks differently[38] and for another, shocks are not evenly
distributed across the country – "the intensity of a stressor
can vary from place to place".[39] What may be a successful
coping strategy in response to a particular stressor in one
community might not be enough to cope with this same
stressor in another community if the latter is experiencing
more intensified adversity. This is not to say that struggling
communities cannot learn from and emulate, to an extent,
more resilient communities, but to suggest that attempts
to increase resilience among struggling communities must
recognise the nuanced and complex phenomenon that is
community resilience, and avoid attempting to use factors
identified in some areas as aiding community resilience as a
magic quick-fix to counter all types and intensities of adversity
in all communities.

A further note on this point concerns the relative 'fragility'
of resilience. Research conducted in resilient communities
highlights that residents were concerned that "the interwoven
fabric of factors supporting community resilience could easily
fray...if local facilities and amenities closed, active individuals
withdrew...or the area experienced rapid population change".[40]
Rather than resilient communities "journey[ing] from a
position of insecurity...to stability and strength...community
resilience is actually a fragile state and the fabric of factors
supporting resilience requires ongoing maintenance".[41]
Alongside not viewing the factors associated with resilient
communities as a quick-fix to be blanket-applied to all other
communities regardless of individual circumstances, resilience
needs to be understood as a long-term process requiring
continual work and effort. As Nick Wilding writes in a report
by the Carnegie UK Trust, "resilience and vulnerability are two

sides of one coin"[42]. That is, resilience and vulnerability are not mutually exclusive and communities evidencing resilience in relation to one shock can embody vulnerability in relation to another in the future if resilience is not practiced and constantly sought after.

1   Ann S Masten, *Ordinary Magic: Resilience in Development* (London: The Guildford Press, 2014), p. 5.

2   Ibid.

3   Ibid., p. 16; Ann S Masten, 'Resilience in developing systems: Progress and promise as the fourth wave rises', *Development and Psychopathology* 19, (2007) pp. 921-930 (p. 922).

4   Masten, *Ordinary Magic* (2014) p. 9.

5   Deborah Platts-Fowler and David Robinson, 'Community resilience: a policy tool for local government?', *Local Government Studies* 42, 5 (2016) pp. 762-784 (p. 766); Susan Christopherson, Jonathan Michie and Peter Tyler, 'Regional resilience: theoretical and empirical perspectives', *Cambridge Journal of Regions, Economy and Society*, 3, 1 (2010) pp. 3-10 (p. 3).

6   Christopherson et al., 'Regional resilience' (2010) p. 3.

7   C S Holling (1996) Cited in Christopher B Barrett and Mark A Constas, 'Toward a theory of resilience for international development applications', *PNAS*, 111, 40 (2014) pp. 14,625-14,630 (p. 14,625).

8   Humanitarian Emergency Response Review (2011) p. 16, assets.publishing. service.gov.uk/government/uploads/system/uploads/attachment_data/ file/67579/HERR.pdf

9   Ibid.

10 Ungar (2008) cited in Platts-Fowler and Robinson, 'Community resilience' (2016) p. 10.

11 Lena Weingartner and Florence Pichon with Catherine Simonet, *How self-help groups strengthen resilience: a study of Tearfund's approach to tackling food insecurity in protracted crises in Ethiopia* (2017) p. 10 www.odi.org/sites/odi.org.uk/files/ resource-documents/11625.pdf

12 Bob Hansford, *Roots: reducing the risk of disaster in our communities*, in Helen Gaw, ed., 2nd edn, (Teddington: Tearfund, 2011) p. 9.

13 Christopherson et al., 'Regional resilience' (2010) p. 5.

14 BT, *Civil resilience: Who we are*. www.btplc.com/CivilResilience/Whoweare/ index.htm

15 Humanitarian Emergency Response Review (2011) p. 16.

16 Nick Wilding, *Exploring Community Resilience in times of rapid change* (Fiery Spirits Community of Practice supported by Carnegie UK Trust, 2011) p. 8.

17 The Global Resilience Network cited in Wilding, *Exploring Community Resilience* (2011) p. 8.

18 Ron Martin et al, 'How regions react to recessions: resilience and the role of economic structure', *Regional Studies*, 50, 4 (2016), pp. 561-585 (p. 581).

19 Platts-Fowler and Robinson, 'Community resilience' (2016) p. 6.

20 Platts-Fowler and Robinson, *Neighbourhood Resilience in Sheffield* (2013) p. i.

21 Ibid., p. 22.

22 Ibid., p. 18.

23 Christopherson et al., 'Regional resilience' (2010) p. 7.

24 Platts-Fowler and Robinson, *Neighbourhood Resilience in Sheffield* (2013) p. 20.

25 Cinderby et al., *Practical action to build community resilience* (2014) p. 4.

26 Jonathan Joseph, 'Resilience as embedded neoliberalism: a governmentality approach', *Resilience*, 1, 1 (2013) pp. 38-52.

27 Lee Gregory, *Trading time: Can exchange lead to social change?* (Bristol: Policy Press, 2015) p. 123.

28 Deborah Platts-Fowler and David Robinson, 'Community resilience: a policy tool for local government?' *Local Government Studies* 42, 5 (2016) pp. 762-784 (p. 3).

29 Refugee Studies Centre, *Local Faith Communities and Resilience in Humanitarian Situations* (2013) p. 3. www.rsc.ox.ac.uk/files/files-1/wp90-local-faith-communities-resilience-2013.pdf

30 Ibid.

31 Cinderby et al., *Practical action to build community resilience* (2014) p. 4.

32 Yolanda Dreyer, 'Community resilience and spirituality – keys to hope for a post-apartheid South Africa' *Pastoral Psychology*, 64, 5 (2015), pp. 651-662 (p. 657); Refugee Studies Centre, *Local Faith Communities* (2013) p. 1.

33 Chloe Quanrud and Catriona Dejean, *Inspiring Change: Impact and Learning Report* (Tearfund, 2016) p. 16.

34 Refugee Studies Centre, *Local Faith Communities* (2013) p. 2.

35 Ibid., p. 3.

36 See Pendall et al (2010) cited in Christopherson et al., 'Regional resilience' (2010) p. 7.

37 Ibid. p. 9.

38 Platts-Fowler and Robinson, 'Community resilience' (2016) p. 12.

39 Platts-Fowler and Robinson, *Neighbourhood Resilience in Sheffield* (2013) p. 10.

40 Platts-Fowler and Robinson, 'Community resilience' (2016) p. 28.

41 Ibid.

42 Wilding, *Exploring Community Resilience* (2011) p. 28.